CLAYTON HALL.

HISTORICAL AND DESCRIPTIVE

NOTICES

OF

DROYLSDEN,

Past and Present.

BY JOHN HIGSON,

AUTHOR OF "THE GORTON HISTORICAL RECORDER," ETC.

DIDSBURY   MANCHESTER
ENGLAND

ISBN 0 85972 015 2

Printed and Bound in Great Britain
by
THE SCOLAR PRESS LTD
59/61 East Parade
Ilkley
Yorkshire

TO

JOSEPH HADWEN, ESQ.,

OF AUDENSHAW,

PRESIDENT OF THE DROYLSDEN EDUCATIONAL INSTITUTION,

AS A

TRIFLING ACKNOWLEDGMENT,

OF HIS

ATTENTION TO OUR PUBLIC INSTITUTIONS,

𝕮𝖍𝖎𝖘 𝖘𝖒𝖆𝖑𝖑 𝕷𝖔𝖈𝖆𝖑 𝖁𝖔𝖑𝖚𝖒𝖊 𝖎𝖘 𝖎𝖓𝖘𝖈𝖗𝖎𝖇𝖊𝖉,

WITH THE MOST

LIVELY SENTIMENTS OF RESPECT AND ESTEEM,

BY THE AUTHOR.

TABLE OF CONTENTS.

PREFACE.

———•◇•———

IT has long been my earnest desire to publish an historical
and descriptive account of Droylsden, a place now endeared
to me by many pleasant associations, which have sprung up
during a residence of more than twelve years.

Unfortunately for this fancy, Droylsden has scarcely been
named at all by any of our local topographers or county
historians ; yet, though more than ordinary difficulties had
to be encountered, an attempt has been made to record, in
a popular and entertaining style, the past annals of the
township, and to illustrate the manners, customs, and superstitions of its inhabitants. With this design in view, and
for the purpose of investing the locality with as much anti-
quarian and historical interest as possible, no opportunity
has been omitted of eliciting information from either books,
MSS., or aged inhabitants.

Pains have been taken, even at the risk of repetition,
to render each subject as complete and independent as
possible, and also to avoid the tedium consequent on dates
and matter-of-fact details. Still, in every case where a
likelihood seemed to exist of disputes arising hereafter,
the date has been given, though after collation and in-
quiry where conflicting statements existed.

After due allowance for limited time and means has
been made, everything available has been done, it is believed, necessary to render this a useful and trustworthy

book of reference on all matters of importance connected
with Droylsden, past and present. Nevertheless, want of
space and acquaintance precludes full accounts of several
interesting subjects; and the incomplete notices, rather
than satisfy, will indicate to the future student and
literateur what remains to be done.

Obligations for kind assistance are due to John Har-
land, Esq., F.A.S.; the Rev. Canon Raines, of Milnrow;
and the Rev. P. Thompson, B.A., Messrs. F. C. Mallalieu,
Samuel Lees, Peter Etchells, James Birch (assistant overseer), and other Droylsden friends; and also to the
following venerable oral chroniclers :—Messrs. Samuel
Arrandale and John Barlow, especially; Messrs. Benjamin
Bertenshaw, William Holland, Robert Grimshaw, and the
late John Schofield, James Baguley, and James Wild.

Sincere thanks are given to my numerous subscribers
for their encouragement to this endeavour to supply a
cheap and comprehensive history of the township.

And, in conclusion, I must express my gratitude to
Mr. J. B. Coughtrie, of Manchester, for enabling me to
present the truthful and spirited etching of Clayton
Hall, which forms the frontispiece to this work.

JOHN HIGSON.

St. Mary's View, Droylsden,
   July. 1859.

THE
HISTORY OF DROYLSDEN.

———◆———

THE township of Droylsden has been singularly neglected by local topographists and county historians, who seem to have considered the place as either too uninviting or too insignificant to do more more than drop a hint or two of its bare existence. It is not particularly described either in Whitaker's "Manchester," or in Baines's "Lancashire"; Dr. Hibbert Ware gives no special notice; and it is merely enumerated in Gastrell's "Notitia Cestriensis." It does not appear in any of the surveys; nor in the "Extent of the Manor f Manchester," in 1322; nor in the concise history of the manor, written by Sir Oswald Mosley for Corry's "Lancashire." Corry, however, does condescend a special description, probably derived from some county map without his ever having set a foot in its precincts; for he thus summarily disposes of it :—"The village of Droylsden consists of a few irregularly built tenements." Certainly, he also hazards a supplementary account of Fairfield, double the length of that accorded to the township generally; but then that settlement has usually found grace in the sight of compilers of the local directories, &c.

Again, Droylsden can boast of no old ecclesiastical foundation, no "time honoured fane," around which the history of the place has silently, but surely entwined itself; for in by-gone days the place was never deemed of any importance, arising partly from its seclusion, consequent on its being untraversed by any direct road from Manchester, and partly from the hungry, barren nature of its soil—so stiff and unyielding that only laborious attention could render it at all productive.

And, lastly, Time has well nigh obliterated every vestige
of antiquity. Almost the only relic, and even that shorn of
primeval dignity, stands Clayton Hall, once stately in fabric
and sullen in isolation, being approachable only by a
drawbridge over the moat.

LOCATION.

Droylsden is a village and township, pleasantly situated
on the southern bank of the Medlock, and about four miles
east from Manchester, of which parish, civilly, it constitutes
the eastern verge, and abuts on the parish of Ashton-under-
Lyne. It forms, also, a component part of the Poor Law
Union of Ashton-under-Lyne, the magisterial division of
the same name, the county division polling-district of Manchester, the representative and assize division of South
Lancashire, and the hundred of Salford. For purposes
ecclesiastical Droylsden is situated within the Deanery,
Archdeaconry, and Diocese of Manchester, the Archbishop-
rick of York, and, in accordance with the act known as
Sir Robert Peel's, has been constituted a new, separate, and
distinct parish.

BOUNDARIES.

Although the boundaries have never been officially perambulated within memory, yet, by the late Ordnance
survey, they were ascertained with accuracy, and permanently defined and recorded. Beginning at the south-west
verge, Droylsden is separated on the south from Openshaw
by Skerrat's Brook as far as Edge-lane, then obliquely by
that highway to its junction with Moor-lane, and thence
by hedgerows to Seventhorns' Brook, a little south of
Fairfield.   From that point Droylsden is divided from
Audenshaw—first by ascending the brook to Ashton Hill-
lane; then by that highway to Fletcher-lane, late William-
son-lane; next by that lane, and afterwards by hedgerows
and dykes across the Moss to Moor-side Farm, or Far-end-
o'th'-world, where Droylsden juts into Ashton parish.
Formerly the boundary line across the Moss, before its
reclamation and allotment to adjoining estates, was indicated
by long oaken poles, fixed upright at distances of from

twenty to thirty yards apart. Traversing the northern boundary, Droylsden is still divided from Audenshaw by the Lum, or Lumb Brook, until it arrives at Waterside. Hence the river separates the township, first from Failsworth, and then from Newton Heath as far as Bankbridge, where Droylsden crosses the river, and is separated from the same township by the footpath leading towards Philip's Park. Formerly, the only road to this semi-detached plot lay through the river, through which the produce was carted. Leaving the Medlock at the north-west verge of the hamlet of Clayton, first hedgerows, then an arm of the canal, and lastly hedgerows again, part Droylsden from Bradford until the starting point is regained. Little Droylsden, a small insulated portion of the township, once intersected by the old road from Manchester to Ashton, adjoins Gorton, and is almost surrounded by Openshaw.

TOPOGRAPHY AND LOCALITIES.

The township comprises three separate divisions, each having its reputed boundaries—viz., Droylsden Proper, or "Big Droylsden"; Clayton, which adjoins it on the west; and Little Droylsden, which is excised by the intervention of Openshaw.

Droylsden Proper is nominally subdivided into four hamlets—Fairfield, Edge Lane, Greenside, and Castle. Clayton is co-extensive with the ancient demesne, and contains the inferior hamlets of East End and West End. Little Droylsden is not quite two acres in extent, and is said to have once been extra-parochial, enjoying immunity from rates and taxes; but a reference to the town's books proves its assessment to the burdens of the township generally for a century past; and its own title deeds, in 1663, consider it without reservation as an integral portion of Droylsden. Its dependance on Droylsden, though detached from it, is popularly accounted for by a tradition, whereof several conflicting versions are extant, and of which the substance, if there be any, is something like the following. Some five centuries ago, Sir John Byron pensioned an aged domestic with the gift of this small freehold, and she subsequently took up her residence in the cottage appurtenant. One cold frosty morning, says the legend, the chances of the chase leading Sir John Byron in that direction, the grateful recipient of his bounty invited him to a warm posset, a dainty of which he was immoderately fond. The courteous knight alighted from his steed, and whilst partaking of the repast casually inquired in what township she lived. The dame replying, "In none," he asked her in which she should like to be located—in Gorton, Openshaw, or Droylsden. Perhaps out of deference to her old master, or anxious to while away the remainder of her life within the precints of that township where her earlier years had been passed, she promptly replied, " In Droylsden." " Then you shall," says her powerful visitor, who forthwith caused the incorporation of that outlying tenement with Droylsden township. But apart from tradition, a suggestion occurs, that as Gorton snatches from Openshaw one field on the north side of the Corn Brook, or Gorton Brook, which, with this exception, constitutes the boundaries of the townships, so also Little Droylsden may have been wrung* from Openshaw. These two excepted plots may have formed portions of the Openshaw Moss, wherein, in 1322, the tenants of the Lord of Gorton, Openshaw, and Ardwick, and the Lord of Ancoats, had common of turbary, and whereof Sir John Byron had appropriated to himself forty acres of moor. Perhaps when the peat on some of his Ancoats allotments became exhausted, the Byrons, then owning no property either in Gorton or Openshaw, annexed the cleared or residuary land to some Droylsden holding, and thereby it became affiliated to the township. Still the title deed of 1663 mentions Marie Hunt, in conjunction with Sir John Byron, both deceased, as having sometime defined the size and locale of the moss room appertaining to that estate. This connection of a female with the tenement seems to afford some countenance to the old tradition.

---

* A locality named *Wrang* is mentioned, in 1505, in connection with Droylsden Moor and Openshaw.

ORTHOGRAPHY.

In early times, as appears from ancient documents, the orthography of the township was very irregular and unsettled, every scribe, in a most arbitrary way, seeming to spell it as it pleased him ; and it did not always please him to spell it the same way. Hence, in the same document, there are frequently found several variations, as many as five occurring in a legal instrument of 1581. Nearly thirty* changes, or derivations, have been registered ; nor do these transmutations, it is believed, include every modification of the word. Generally speaking, in the olden time there was a large superabundance of letters employed ; with one exception, however, "Drylsden," as found in evidences *temp.* James I., and which probably may satisfy the greatest stickler for phonetic brevity. Till within a comparatively recent period the authorised orthography was "Droylesden," when the elision of the second vowel (e) in the first syllable left the mode of spelling as now fixed and current. But even yet the popular spelling of non-residents is far from settled, as witness the epistolary directions passing through the post, where scores of anomalous excruciations have been observed.

DERIVATION OF NAME.

The designation of the township is of good old Saxon extraction, and seemingly unique, Dresden being its nearest known approach.

Apparently one Dreol, the first colonist, prefixed his own cognomen to a word descriptive of a natural feature of the site ; *den* being simply a territorial appellation for a narrow valley, or wooded dingle, and not like *ham*, *ton*, and *wick*, which imply both settled occupation and inhabitance. *Den* has many variations—dean, dene, deyne, dane, don,

---

* Droysdale, Droylsdale, Droilsdale, Drilesdale, Striledale, Stryledale, Strylesdale, Aroisdale, Droylsdon, Drillesdon, Droylsdane, Drevelesden, Drulsden, Drilsden, Droidsden, Droisden, Drisden, Draylesden, Droylesden, Drilesden, Droilesden, Droilsden, Droyslden, Droylden, Drylisden, Drylesden, Drylsden, and Droylsden.

down, &c., some of which occur in the names of adjacent localities. Ar*den*, in Bredbury; *Den*shawbank, in *Den*ton; *Danes*, in Gorton; *Dane*head, in Au*den*shaw; and *Dane*, in Droylsden. Also, in the reign of Edward I., the boundaries of Clayton are described as "beginning from Har*dene*, passing along the margin of Drulsden (Droylsden), edging close to the ground of Sinderland, and terminating at the demesne lands of Hardene again." From the meagre enumeration of boundary marks, the situation of Hardene is now untraceable, and cannot, specifically, be assigned as within either Openshaw or Bradford, but most likely appertained to the latter. There was also an estate named Clay*den*, divided from Beswick by the river Medlock.

Den has very many etymologies. Kemble, in his "Saxons in England," gives several meanings to the word. "*Den* (A.S.)," says he, "signifies a forest, or outlying pasture in the woods; *den* (Celtic), a small valley, or dingle. Names of places ending in *den* (neuter) always denoted pasture, usually for swine" —that is, *cubile ferarum*, or the *den—lair—abode of wild beasts, animals;* or pasture, &c. "*Denu* (fem.), a valley [a British, and not a Saxon word], is very rarely, perhaps never, found in composition."

Reilly, in his "History of Manchester," says the Saxon *dene* comes from the Celtic *dion* or *din*, which signifies, in Irish and Gaelic, any sheltered neighbourhood, whether protected by the earth or capable of affording cover from a storm—a valley, or whatever is sheltered from illegal practices by any fence. The Anglo-Saxons adopted this word from their Celtic neighbours in both acceptations. The word *dene* also appears to have had a more limited interpretation, and to have meant a particular kind of valley, or dale, enclosed on both sides with hills, and often exhibiting woods, and streams of water convenient for cattle. This restricted meaning is exemplified in the *dene* at Edinburgh; Deansgate, in Manchester and Bolton; St. Mary's Dene, now called Dene, near Bolton; Healey Dene, near Rochdale; Northenden, in Cheshire, &c.

Arden, meaning great wood, is the name of a French

forest, and also of Whitaker's supposed Manchester forest. Still the term *dene*, in its local accceptation, indicates a narrow wooded valley, whose banks rise less abruptly than those of a cleft, or clough, and, in addition to a stream at the bottom, is furnished with a small strip of flat alluvial land lying on its margin. In this sense *den* or *dene* (Anglo-Saxon) is rendered by the late John Just, of Bury, a competent etymological authority, and therefore, as before stated, the most plausible deduction suggests "Dreol 's woody vale," and there is a valley answering to this description near Sunnybank, and another at Waterside.

Clayton apparently refers to the kind of soil around the enclosed *ton*, *tun* (A.S.), space, hamlet, or settlement. Fairfield is the pleasing or beautiful field ; Greenside the locale beside the common or green, and in contradistinction to Moorside, in the vicinity of the Moss. Edge Lane, East End, and West End refer to particular portions of Clayton demesne Castle ; the present designation of a hamlet was once applied distinctively to the house now occupied by John Lowe, and built by Joseph Nicholson about sixty years ago. When inebriated, he invariably proclaimed his intention of travelling in the Netherlands, and some of his neighbours jocularly dubbed his new house "Netherlands Castle," which in time was abbreviated to "Th' Castle," and in that form has been perpetuated.

STRATA, MINERALS, SOILS, ETC.

The contour of the township varies but little. On the south or south-east, it is nearly flat, whilst the soil under cultivation, resting on a stiff clayey substratum, though altered by successive agricultural operations, has doubtless once formed part of, or been covered by, a peaty deposit. On the north side the surface undulates, and the mould, a graft deep, is lighter in colour, and rests on a cold stiff clay, with underlaying beds of sand, rising sometimes to within a few feet of the surface. The westerly portion, except that it lies nearly on the level, exhibits the like characteristics. The eastern division is chiefly flat, with peat or blackmoor-earth resting on clay.

Geologically speaking, the township is principally located on what technically is termed a *fault*, but, more properly speaking, a dislocation in the Manchester coalfield. As stated by Mr. Binney, in his interesting paper on the "Geology of Manchester and its Vicinity," published in the first volume of the "Transactions of the Manchester Geological Society," the prevailing geological character of the township is the upper new red sandstone, with beds of diluvial clay and sand, or gravel near the river, super-imposed. The western edge of an outlying strip, or band, of the upper new red sandstone, which intervenes between the coalfields of Manchester and Denton, Ashton, and Oldham, enters the township from the south, near Openshaw Church, passing through Clayton to Bankbridge Dyeworks, a little to the east of which it was penetrated ninety-eight yards. The eastern edge is believed to range under Gorton Reservoir, by Fairfield, to a little west of Medlock Vale. At Clayton-Bridge it was found fifty-nine yards thick, lying upon the red marls. These marls, generally known as "red raddle," intermixed with limestone, were found by the late Mr. Bradbury in Jericho Clough, fifty-one yards four inches thick, and resting on the lower new red sandstone; and, near Medlock Vale, the same gentlemen found the lower new red sandstone sixteen yards thick, and resting on the coal measures.

The coals of Clayton, Bradford, and Collyhurst form what is called the Manchester coalfield, and are probably an elevated mass, entirely surrounded by the new red sandstone. Seven beds of the Bradford and Clayton mines have been worked. They are named respectively Charlotte, Three Quarters, Four Feet, Yard, New, Doctor, and Two Feet Mines. In Clayton there are two shafts of an average depth of 145 yards, and the produce is suitable only for engine fuel. Their annual rateable value to the poor is £145 16s. 8d., which realises £7 15s., out of which Droylsden township has to refund £3 7s. 7d. to Bradford, as most, if not all, of the coals are now obtained underneath that township.

Clayton has formed the boundary of coals worked in

Droylsden, and easterly thence the strata are greatly disturbed, and the coal, if any exist, appear from various trials to be depressed beneath the sandstone to an immense depth.

This sandy deposit, so frequently referred to, is doubtless of sedimentary or water origin, from whence and the geological outlines of the district, Mr. Binney, in his concluding remarks, conjectures that Clayton, Bradford, &c., once formed an island, and that a strait, now the site of Droylsden, Openshaw, Gorton, and other places, intervened between the Manchester coalfield and that of Denton and Oldham. In these waters the currents seem to have flowed with very different velocities, as evinced by the coarse-grained sand of the lower red sandstone, the comminuted mud of the red marls with limestone, the fine sand mixed with large pebbles of the upper red sandstone, and the fine-grained silt of the upper red marls.

The mineral earths are few. Alum slate has been procured from the Clayton collieries, potters' clay on the Moss, marls everywhere, and indurated clay was formerly obtained at Clayton for the purpose of manufacturing into firebricks.

SCENERY.

Although destitute of prospects which excite wonder and admiration, yet the scenery on the northern side of the township, and especially in the vale of the Medlock, is pleasing and attractive. The first impressions of a stranger will not prove unfavourable to the district, if obtained, on a clear day, from the summit of a cotton mill, from whence the view is both extensive and diversified, exhibiting a succession of fields and hamlets, farmsteads and manufactories, church steeples and tall chimneys. No doubt the aspect of the township has been much changed by progressive agricultural developments, comprising the extinction of forests, the enclosure of moors, and the cultivation of mosses, as also by the formation of roads and the erection of dwellings; yet its general contour remains substantially unimpaired. The river still winds through the vale; but in the lapse of ages, either the volume of water has diminished, or the

stream has sawn its channel deeper into the crust of the
earth. A want of picturesque beauty arises from the absence
of sheltering trees, and also from the lands being mown
or depastured to the exclusion of fields of waving corn;
hence, in summer time, there is a sameness of landscape,
which detracts from the enjoyment of a sweet and refresh-
ing rural walk.

MEANS OF COMMUNICATION AND TRAFFIC.

Roads.—First instituted were footpaths, leading from one
village or hamlet to another, and to the market and parish
church. These by-paths yet form public conveniences for
business, and healthy outlets for invigorating strolls. Probably in Droylsden the earliest bridle lane, or public track-
way for horses, carts being then unknown or uncommon, was
a trunk line, or artery, circuitously connecting Droylsden
with Manchester, either through Newton or Openshaw.
The former road crossed the Medlock near Clayton-Bridge
and the latter near Philip's Park, by means of fords, which
in times of flood were both disagreeable and unsafe. The
ford first named was superseded by a narrow but picturesque
bridge, elevated in the centre, passengers having to ascend
on the one side and descend on the other. In the lapse of
time the river undermined the foundations, when, about
seventy years ago, the present handsome and substantial
structure was erected at the expense of the hundred. The
small adjoining hamlet, long known as the Mill Houses,
has, since the removal of the corn-mill, been popularly
designated Clayton-Bridge, which name has likewise been
appropriated by the railway station hard by.

There was also a singular class of convenience roads,
by which the occupants of one farm possessed the right of
traversing the intervening lands of a neighbour whilst
carting fuel from the Moss.

Formerly, by means of the social pillion, farmers' horses
carried double, and a "horsing stock," or stone, for mounting
purposes, was considered essentially requisite to every farmyard. And thus picturesquely the farmer and his spouse,
chatting like Darby and Joan, trotted to fair, to market, or

chapel, or even to funerals ; a *cortége* of the latter description having once left Droylsden with more than twenty
couples.

The little trade of the district was facilitated by pack-
horse carriers down to near the close of the last century,
when old James Harrison, the last of his class in Droylsden,
dwelt in Greenside-lane. A few years further on, and the
Nicholsons carried goods from Manchester, when, owing to
the badness of the roads, their cart was drawn by four
horses lengthwise, and frequently on Saturday night did not
arrive at Lane Head until eleven or twelve o'clock. Occasionally one wheel of the vehicle was driven along the
ditch, being preferable to the highway from possessing a
firmer bottom.

In addition to the materials now in use for road repairing,
the town's book of a century ago reveals the following curious
items—viz., "Making cob-hills, and plattings, and felling,
leading, and setting up stumps," then deemed indispensable
in road affairs. The time is remembered when, in proportion as material was required, two cottages were pulled
down piecemeal, in order to repair certain lengths of
highway. About that period a large portion of Edge-
Lane was in such "bad fettle" that, whilst passing through
the ruts, the cart wheels sunk up to the axletrees, and the
chest or bottom "hurred," *i.e.* grated, on the pathway
between. The Clayton folks used to repair their length
now and then by filling the ruts with brushwood, and then
pulling the sides on the top of it. In 1786 John Saxon
indicted a certain part of the lane from Clayton-Bridge
to Greenside, the expense of which, £23 10s., was afterwards
refunded from the rates.

But Droylsden boasted a rule without exception ; its roads
were all in an execrable condition. A stranger one day
inquired at the White Hart which was the best way to
Little Moss. "Up the deitch" was the brief and truthful
reply. In fact so foul was the length intervening betwixt
that public-house and Square-fold, that some folk, choosing
"roundabout for th' nearest," trespassed through Round
Oak-meadow, whilst others of a more determined cast of

mind doffed their shoes and stockings and .waded through barefoot. So unequal was the surface in some places, that pedestrians fifty yards in advance of their fellows, frequently appeared to pop over head, and become entirely invisible. One well-known rut or cavity was locally famous as "Jack Hollant Hole," and instead of filling up and rendering it firm, it was customary, when a loaded cart had to pass, to impress a bevy of hatters and weavers, in order as best they could to pull and push it through this "slough of despond."

Turnpike.—Owing principally to narrow, roundabout, and unpaved lane-roads, Droylsden was formerly quite isolated from Manchester. About 1824 the owners of the Clayton estate formed a length of private road extending from the East End to the West End. Subsequently, with a view of cutting a turnpike from Clayton to Ashton-under-Lyne, the North-road was begun by the same parties. Owing to contemplated opposition from the Earl of Stamford and Warrington the design of extension was abandoned, and an act procured, in 1825, whereby the first-named private road was constituted a portion of a new diversion of the road to Ashton, and in the following summer was continued to the old turnpike, in Audenshaw. On an application to Parliament for a renewal of the trust, in 1851, the ratepayers of Droylsden succeeded in modifying the act, by the introduction of a number of Droylsden gentle· men in the reappointment of the trustees. The undertaking has proved highly beneficial to the township by supplying direct communication with Manchester. Commencing in December, 1849, after several fluctuations, and changes of route to the old road, an omnibus plies on the new road, to and from the city, every alternate hour

Railways.—In addition to the facilities for traffic afforded by road and canal, two lines of railway compete for the transit of passengers. The Ashton branch of the Lancashire and Yorkshire Railway was opened April 23, 1846, with a station in the township, designated from the locality, "Lum," but which has since been more properly renamed "Droylsden Station." The Manchester, Sheffield, and Lincolnshire Railway, passing just without the southern boundary of the township, was opened to Ashton-under-Lyne November 17, 1841, with a temporary hut dignified as "Fairfield Station," which has since been replaced with a pleasing erection of stone.

POSTAL ARRANGEMENTS.

The inconvenience of Droylsden's subordination to Audenshaw and the primitive machinery of a foot messenger having been felt keenly, early in 1847 petitions for an improvement were numerously and influentially signed. In the following year, on the 6th of August, the office in Market-street was opened, with one bag received and another despatched every day. Additional advantages since accorded now give three despatches, averaging 150, and two deliveries, averaging 200, letters per day. Monetary and business transactions have been facilitated by the establishment of a Money Order Office on January 2, 1855, which in the first four years issued 2,178, and cashed 1,648 orders.

STREAMS AND INLAND NAVIGATION.

The head waters of the Medlock are gathered into three main or parent streams, rising respectively at Dirtcar and Besom Hill, near Oldham, and Scouthead in Saddleworth.

Meandering past Droylsden, through the pretty vale to which it imparts its name, the river is impressed into service by several extensive bleacheries. The Medlock, usually a shallow stream, is periodically swollen to a considerable magnitude by torrents of rain, which, rushing from the hills, leave valuable gravelly deposits on its margin. Although, within Droylsden, the banks nowhere rise abruptly, yet the channel is sufficiently furrowed to prevent any extensive inundation, the mischief being usually confined to slight floodings ; but at times considerable damage has resulted to the dyeworks at Bankbridge.

Droylsden has excellent water communication, which has chiefly contributed to its present flourishing condition.

The Manchester and Ashton-under-Lyne Canal, begun about 1794, and opened some three years after, with branches to Heaton Norris, Fairbottom, and Hollinwood, has its two main junctions in the township. Facilities are thereby afforded for conveying coals and other commodities to the mills and workshops located on its arms and banks; and public convenience is promoted by several private wharves for the landing or loading of goods.

AREA, EXTENT, ADMEASUREMENT, ETC.

The township is nearly two miles long, and about one and a half broad. Its superficial area was measured by Messrs. Johnson and Son as 1,593 acres; Rickman's computation, in the population returns of 1831, gives 1,400; the Tithe Commissioners, in the last census returns, 1,611; Messrs. Dunn and Wilson's survey, in 1826, exclusive of roads and river, embraces 1,570 acres 2 roods 12 perches; and the Ordnance survey, the most accurate of all, yields 1,621a. 1r. 24p. This gives a surface of rather more than 2½ square miles; consequently Droylsden, in territorial extent, is the seventh of the thirty townships comprising the extensive parish of Manchester.

These discrepancies have been reconciled in a manner similar to that facetiously adopted by a neighbouring agriculturist. Being in treaty for a farm, the owner represented it at a greatly exaggerated size; but the farmer naively remarked that he should not have thought it had been so large, but knew that *wet land would tread out !*

Messrs. Dunn and Wilson surveyed Little Droylsden to 1a. 3r. 37p.; land on the north side of the river to 39p.; and that occupied by the Ashton Canal to 22a. The lengths of the several branches of that navigation are—Manchester and Ashton, 2 miles 140 yards; Hollinwood branch, 1 mile 140 yards; and the Stockport branch, 375 yards. The Lancashire and Yorkshire Railway is 1,445 yards in length, and 11a. 2r. 37p. in area. The river Medlock occupies 6a. 0r. 37p.; the turnpike, 13a. 1r. 27p.; and woods and plantations, 28a.

POPULATION.

From the scanty memorials accessible, apparently during several centuries the township made slight advances both in prosperity and population. In those times, the rearing of a new dwelling—for entire streets were not then built at a single impulse—was an important era in the meagre annals of the place ; and probably there were times when even "the oldest inhabitant" could not recollect the erection of a domicile on a new foundation.

Prior to the rise of the cotton manufacture, the population was very insignificant in number. In 1655 Droylsden contained 32 ratepayers, probably representing less than 200 inhabitants. The earliest authentic, but private, enumeration of the population dates in 1774, at which time the township included within its limits 107 houses, all occupied, and in the aggregate by 111 families, comprising 699 individuals, or little more than the number of workpeople now employed at Droylsden Mills. The erections of the mills brought large accessions of inhabitants, the bulk of whom reside in their vicinity. The following tabulated statement of the several census taken by Government shows the modern progressive increase of population :—

Date	Houses	Families	Males	Females	Total
1801	233		755	797	1552
1811	329	393	1070	1131	2201
1821	397	426	1469	1386	2855
1831	549	547	1476	1520	2996
1841	872		2398	2535	4933
1851	1183		3041	3239	6280

Although, in 1831, the rate of increase per cent of the two previous enumerations (41·8 and 29·7) was not maintained, being only 4·9, yet the progress (64·6) was extremely buoyant in the next ten years, and remained steady, 27·3, in the last census, at which time the density of population was 3·87 persons per acre. In January, 1852, there were 9 inns and public-houses, 23 beer-shops, 52 provision and other shops, 1,023 cottages under £10 rental, and 55 private houses above £10 per year.

LOCAL GOVERNMENT AND PAROCHIAL OFFICERS.

For centuries the maintenance of the peace of the township was vested in the constables, nominated at the annual town's meetings, and confirmed by the magistrates, and slightly aided by the wardens of Newton Chapel, one of the latter being triennially furnished by Droylsden. Since the erection of Droylsden Church, annually, on Easter Monday forenoon, the rector, or incumbent, has always appointed one warden and one sidesman, and the parishioners have elected two corresponding officials. Their external duties embrace perambulatory visits, on Sabbath forenoons, to inns and taverns to guard against "filling" infractions, and also to scour the fields and lanes from persons profaning the day by following their worldly occupations. Droylsden has also its representative sidesman, annually elected at the Cathedral and parish church.

Within memory the only public fabric in the township was the village stocks – the old-fashioned panacea for reforming drunkards and desecraters of the Sabbath. This crazy wooden machine stood on the green at Lane Head, near the present King's Head, and was accidentally burned down with the bonfire one 5th of November. Afterwards, in 1793, at a cost of £3 10s. 9d., the town erected a new pair in front of two thatched cottages, near the Yew Tree, on the green adjacent to the terminus of Ashton Hill-lane. The initials of the current constable, Samuel Beswick, were incised on the upright stone pillars, which were stayed together with an iron bolt near the top. The horizontal boards were perforated for the legs of a couple of inebriates, with provision for a wrist of each person by means of a slot, with hasp and lock appertaining to the inside of each pillar. But no use is recollected to have been made of either of these rude instruments of justice, the last of which was removed some years ago.

Droylsden was included within the jurisdiction of th magisterial division of Ashton-under-Lyne March 1, 1839, and subsequently the protective vigilance of the new police force was introduced, the township being divided into

two districts. A sergeant and officer located in Droylsden
Proper also supervise Little Droylsden, and one officer is
placed at Clayton. Formerly prisoners were taken for
temporary confinement to the Openshaw Lock-up, preparatory to conveyance to Ashton for examination before
the magistrates, two of whom, acting for the county, reside
within Droylsden. A county constabulary station was
erected in 1855, near Victoria Mills. It is a compact brick
edifice, containing separate lock-ups, or cells, for males and
females, with residences on each side for the sergeant and
officer and their families. In addition to the nocturnal
vigilance of the police, a private watchman has always been
maintained in Fairfield, and one each at most of the mills
and manufactories.

The municipal and parochial affairs of the township,
since time immemorial, probably from 1662, have always
been vested in the overseers of the poor, and constables or
surveyors of the highways, annually nominated at the
vestry meetings, and confirmed by the magistrates. When
the Poor-Law Union of Ashton-under-Lyne was formed,
in 1837, Droylsden was included, and annually elects its
representative guardian, and participates in the advantages,
real or presumed, of the new Union Workhouse, erected to
the north of Ashton in 1850, and also in other supposed
benefits of this local centralisation.

The roads, or highways of the township, are repaired by
ratione tenure, and for this purpose, by an arrangement
entered into in some one's days, they are divided by mere
stones into various lengths, which were allotted or attached
to the several farm holdings in the township. Owing,
however, to inexplicable transfers and sales of portions of
estates for building upon, these " statute lengths " are being
periodically divided and subdivided until the responsibility
becomes almost indeterminable. And various assignments
from time to time have been disclaimed, or thrown upon the
town, to the detriment of the ratepayers. The supervision
and control of the roads is vested by annual election in a
board, comprising several *honorary* surveyors, who appoint

one *working* or stipendiary assistant, in order to collect the highway rate, and see to the repair of the respective lengths, or summonses for the neglect.

Resembling Joseph's coat of many colours, every known variety of road-making and cobbling seems to exist, but the primitive methods carry the preponderance. The town's apportionments are an exception, being in a tolerably efficient state of repair, the expense being defrayed by a small annual rate.* And Edmund Buckley, Esq., a few years ago, expended a large sum in thoroughly paving his several lengths; but the remainder, generally, are either badly paved or unpaved, and only now and then repaired with a well-nigh invisible coating of cinders or gravel. An occasional or bi-annual sweeping is given to the Clayton-road, and a little sometimes administered to portions of Market-street and Droylsden-lane; but there are other parts not thoroughly cleansed once in twelvemonths.

Droylsden is comprised within the limits of that useful branch of the judicature, the Ashton County Court, and its privileges have been frequently made use of by the inhabitants.

PAROCHIAL RATES, EXPENDITURE, ETC.

Notwithstanding that the town rented for its own use one house in 1774, and two some six years later, at present there exists neither building nor offices, whether rented or otherwise, for parochial purposes, and a small monetary allowance is made for the use of a room in the New Institute for the weekly attendances of the relieving officer.

The manuscript and documentary property of the ratepayers is principally deposited in a strong oaken chest with three locks, of which the assistant overseer is custodian.

The excellent map and survey of the township, executed by Messrs. Dunn and Wilson in 1826, became the property of Mr. Tinker, when, on behalf of the township, some nine or ten years ago, he furnished three tithe maps, one for transmission to London, another to be deposited in the

---

* The length of highway in the township is about 8,000 yards, of which 1,032 appertain to the town.

Cathedral, and the third for the ratepayers' use, but which now lies in private hands.

In 1655, when Droylsden, for poor-rate purposes, was associated with Manchester, the township possessed 32 assessments, and the rate, for six months ending November 25, amounted to £7 19s. 11d. in the aggregate. The connection with the mother-town, so far as regarded general parochial purposes, was incidentally repealed by the act of Charles II. (1662), under which Droylsden has since been conventionally treated as a distinct and separate parish.

In the reign of William III. (1692), the annual value of the township was £329 17s. 1d., according to the land tax assessment. The yearly value of real property in Droylsden was assessed at £4,896 in 1814, and the subsequent assessments to the county-rate have been as follow :—£4,955, in 1815 ; £6,811, in 1829 ; £12,900, in 1841 ; and £16,902, in 1853, the last undertaken.

The tithes of Droylsden and Clayton are enumerated, in 1556, 1578, and 1635, amongst the endowment sources in the charters of the Collegiate Church. In 1701 the warden and fellows leased the tithes of Droylsden for £11 15s. to James Hall, and they received also £5 10s. for those of Clayton demesne. In 1848, the tithes of the township entire realised £97 for the Dean and Canons of Manchester.

The cost of repairing the township's highways was once defrayed from the constable's lay, to which, in 1759, fifty-four persons paid sums ranging from 3d. to £2, amounting to £8 0s. 0½d. in the whole. Nineteen years later, four lays of this description raised, within the twelvemonth, £32 0s. 8d., which amount was increased to £33 1s. 2d. by the collection from the cottages. The disbursements comprised £14 9s. 9½d. for money warrants and incidental expenses, £9 16s. 7d. for repairing the highways, and £3 13s. 6d. arrears on that score, leaving the sum of £5 1s. 3½d as a balance in hand. Eight years subsequently, the assessments had increased to seventy, and the rate deducible therefrom was £17 6s. 5½d., at sixpence in the pound.

In 1732, the Droylsden quarterly assessment realised

£8 4s. 11¼d. for the poor, at the rate of 6d. in the pound. In 1847, the gross estimated rental was £10,915, on which £618 8s. 8d. was produced by a one shilling rate. In May, 1858, the gross estimated rental was £20,023 8s. 10d., the rateable value £16,855 11s. 2d.; and the poor-rate, at 1s. 6d. in the pound, was £1,158 3s., of which £334 13s. 9d. was paid by the owners under the Small Tenements Act.

The entire parochial rates were returned in 1828-9 at £333, and ten years later this amount was only exceeded by £30.

Formerly there were several greens, or plots of unclaimed land, in the township, and large strips of waste along the lane sides; latterly, these have been mostly enclosed, and in some cases a monetary equivalent has been yielded to the town. Instances are said to exist of cottages having been erected on the waste, and their owners being destitute of any original title deed or evidence.

Under the old local system the ratepayers are found regaling themselves with drink at a town's meeting, and paying for it out of the poor-rate; bearing the expenses of "askings," weddings, and christenings, purchasing Godfrey's cordial, and physic, and paying for *post mortem* examinations, coffins, and burials, from the same source; paying the paupers by the "long," or calendar, month, in contradistinction to the lunar one; allowing 2s. per week to a "nonwit," or idiot child; binding an apprentice *for life*, at an expense of £3 4s.; searching the town for rogues and vagrants, at a charge of 2s.; fetching back runaway apprentices; paying for loom hire, and numbering, writing, swearing-in, and bounty for, militia; also subscribing towards Brindle Workhouse and the Manchester Infirmary; making allowances to passengers, tramps, or vagrants; losing by light gold and bad silver; purchasing in two years, 1817 and 1818, at a bonus of one halfpenny each, more than two thousand sparrow's heads; and buying sundry articles of furniture and clothing for the paupers— such as shifts, petticoats, rockets (frocks), and bedgowns for the females; and shirts, waistcoats, breeches, and jackets, for the males; as, also, bedstocks, straw and chaff beds, with the usual clothing; chairs, tables, and firegrates—the latter then provided by the tenant, and not, as now, by the landlord.

In those " good old times" many a fracas occurred at the town's meeting to break the monotony of the scene. A refractory overseer has refused to deliver up his books and accounts, and an appeal to the strong arm of the law having proved unavailing, an enraged ratepayer, of indomitable courage and strength, takes the matter in his own hands, and, in the midst of the assembly, flies at the obstinate official, downs him in real Lancashire style, and wrests the coveted documents from his grasp!

Under the system of poor-law unions, the parochial affairs and expenditure are conducted uniformly on principles both useful and economical. But the town's meetings, from having less control over pecuniary matters, have become sectional and exclusive, and especially since the time of holding them—two o'clock in the afternoon—is utterly at variance with the convenience of the great bulk of ratepayers, who are engaged in the staple employment of the village. Added to which, through the application of the Small Tenement Act, the majority of ratepayers are deprived of the privilege of voting on parochial affairs. An attempt to popularise town's meetings by holding them at six in the evening partially succeeded a few years ago; but, in obedience to the powers that be, they have reverted to the ancient rule, which, like the laws of the Medes and Persians, altereth not.

HISTORICAL NOTICES.

The early history of the township is involved in impenetrable obscurity. Whitaker conjectures that, five centuries prior to the Christian era, the parish of Manchester was a wild, unfrequented woodland, the domain of birds and beasts. Many indications of this ancient forest are still discernable, and especially in the names of fields and localities. The finding in the moss of a stone celt— *i.e.* a hammer or spear head—now unfortunately lost, probably identifies the locality with the temporary sojourn of the ancient Britons, during the era known as the stone period.

Droylsden is connected with the Roman conquest, if not by occupation, by means of three coins, now in the possession of Miss Piccope, who resides on the Moss. They were exhumed about seventeen years ago, whilst making a deep ditch or trench amongst some knolls, or undulations, in order to reclaim a portion of the morass now attached to the farm at the Castle, held by Mrs. Alice Howarth. They lay without any protection on the natural mould or clay, and scattered about were fragments of coarse earthenware, gone soft from exposure to the damp soil. There was also an implement, now lost, described as a " tommahawk," or small-sized hatchet of bell metal (perhaps bronze), with a wooden haft, or handle, preserved by the anti-septic properties of the peat.

The following description of the coins is supplied by a numismatical friend :—No. 1. Trajan (A.D. 98-117), second brass, obverse, laureated head to the right ; reverse, a figure seated—legends on both sides defaced. No. 2. Antoninus Pius (A.D. 138-161), second brass, obverse, much corroded, head to the right ; reverse, a female figure standing with something in each hand (perhaps Genius, with Hasta and Cornucopia); S.C., in the field, for Senatus Consultum ; and of the legend only the word " cos " can be read, that part of the coin following this word being cut or broken away. No. 3. Aurelius (A.D. 161-180), second brass, obverse, defaced ; reverse, a priest sacrificing at an altar, with the S.C.; legend, TR . . . . COS II., showing the coin to be struck when the Emperor was a second time consul.

Of the foundation of Droylsden no information exists in either authentic record or the voice of tradition. On the formation of the Saxon parish of Manchester in the year 446, this then probably nameless district, as well as the present parish of Ashton-under-Lyne, was included therein. About a century after, the Saxon kingdom of Deira was established, and comprehended the extensive parish of Manchester. The name of the township indisputably associates it with Saxon origin, and its connection with this colonising, agricultural people is further strengthened by a reference to the names of fields and enclosures, many of them handed down intact from that period. Whitaker, on presumptive evidence doubtless, conjectures Droylsden to have been colonised about the year 610, when, he states, the Saxon pioneers disencumbered the land of its ancient oaks. At that period, it is not speculative to suppose the surface of the district composed of woodland and marsh. First comes the erection of wattled lath and plaster huts and homesteads for the new comers; then the surface drainage of the soil by gutters and ditches, outlets into the brooks and river; the fencing-off and enclosure of meadow, arable, and pasture land; and hence the recurrence of the appellative "heys," meaning, primarily, hedges or enclosures fenced off from the forest.

Of the Danish irruptions about 870, there are dim traditions yet extant, as well as of the final overthrow of those predatory incursionists in these parts some half century later. [The substance of these lingering legends may be found in the "Gorton Historical Recorder," pp. 44-5.]

About 1070, Manchester was created a manor, and Droylsden formed a component portion. The ravages of the Northmen or Danes, and the desolating policy of the Conqueror, may partly account for the omission of Droylsden and other neighbouring hamlets or townships in the Doomsday survey of the kingdom, which was undertaken (1080-6) at his command.

Droylsden first emerges from obscurity when the Claytons resided at Clayton Hall. In the twelfth century they owned the greater portion of the lands in the township, inclusive of the villeins who cultivated the soil. Their successors, the Byrons, possessed a sort of MS. chartulary, or book, called "The Blacke Boke of Clayton," into which, from time to time, were copied all the deeds and documents pertaining to the various estates of the family. This interesting register now lies amongst the "Townley Collection" in the British Museum. From the first authentic mention in 1199, further notice of the township is not upon record, except in connection with the Byrons, for many generations afterwards.

When the parish of Ashton-under-Lyne was carved or parcelled out of the spacious parish of Manchester (anterior to 1291), Droylsden became a frontier township in the ancient parish, as it remains, civilly, to this day.

The annals of the place for a long period continue locked up, incidentally, in the Byron muniments, and the evidences and title deeds of more modern proprietors. Little apparent alteration, it is presumed, took place in the general appearance of the village, if the term be allowable, during the lapse of many successive centuries.

Formerly Droylsden could not boast of any grouping or concentration of dwellings worthy of the epithet of village or hamlet. But scattered over an area of more than two and a half square miles, and nestling amongst the hedgerow trees bordering the lanes and thoroughfares, straggling here and there, were isolated farmsteads, interspersed with a few, very few, detached cottages, planted, like angels' visits, far between.

The inhabitants were not prone to change. Empires and states might rise and fall, influxions of settlers might elsewhere occur, but here, in this secluded nook, the same family stock inhabited the same dwelling, may be, for generations. Occasionally, the off-shoots erected a new dwelling, but more frequently migrated to Manchester, or other places, where the means of livelihood were more abundant. Hence, with scarcely the intrusion of a single interloper, the same family names were permanently transmitted, until the place became quite a nest of Booths, Grimshaws, Halls, Hibberts, Nicholsons, Oldhams, Thorps, Travises, &c.

The second colonisation was a manufacturing one, begun with the erection of Fairfield, which, like Clayton Hall aforetime, for a while constituted the metropolis of the township, but which, in turn, through the new-born vigour of Droylsden Proper, has again relapsed into a suburb. The real manufacturing settlement, however, was effected through the erection of the mills. Many of the earlier operatives migrated from Stockport; others have followed from surrounding villages and towns, many from Ireland, some from Derbyshire, and others even from the button manufacturing districts of Gloucestershire. These various elemental grafts add vigour to the mass; but, owing to their comparatively recent location, are not yet thoroughly amalgamated. And, as yet, there are few small capitalists, the status of the entire population being nearly on a par.

In the present state of society the indigenous Droylsdenian is submerged beneath the new blood, which represents the progress of the place as exemplified in its social, intellectual, and religious movements. The old aboriginals, tenaciously clinging to their ancient habits, still adhere to farming and the hand-loom, and a few to hatting. Generally speaking, they stand proudly or sullenly aloof from the mills, and few instances are known of their rising into managers, bookkeepers, overlookers, and other superior situations, all these being filled, well nigh without exception, by those who are foreign to the soil. On the influx of operatives, the "old originals" were most active in their antagonism, and, if persecution could have repelled the new comers, then their efforts would have met with success. Many of them still retain their former exclusiveness, and seldom intermix with the interlopers, just as the "Castle bulldogs" and "Little Moss gawbies," though inhabiting adjoining hamlets in Droylsden and Audenshaw, yet remain distinct races, especially the young folks, who refuse to associate in their recreations, and seldom, if ever, intermarry. There is a sort of clanship amongst them; they court the friendship of few outsiders, and if you offend one, you offend all.

CLAYTON HALL.

Clayton Hall, which imparted a name to a family seated here in the twelfth century, is located about three miles east from Manchester, and confers appellation on a hamlet which forms the western portion of the township of Droylsden. The mansion, situated on a slightly rising ground, near the midst of an ample demesne, boasting as many broad

c

Lancashire "acres as there are days i'th' year," was, in accordance with the prudence or jealousy of past times, encompassed with a broad and deep moat, once crossed by means of a drawbridge, since replaced by an elegant and permanent stone structure of two arches. This ancient environment is fed by a running stream, and encloses a quadrangular area of about two statute acres. The original Hall, having been erected during a turbulent period of English history, was doubtless castellated and loop-holed, with tower, courtyard, &c. But the present homely pile consists of two buildings in a line, of different periods, the oldest being of timber and plaster, and of a date, apparently, subsequent to the desertion of the Byrons. Its southern end is surmounted with a wooden turret containing the bell. Tradition represents that Humphrey Cheetham removed a portion of the structure, with the intention of rebuilding it on a more extensive scale, and, afterwards abandoning the design, he merely erected the the other insignificant portion, which is, apparently, a work of the seventeeth century. The front aspect looks westerly. On all other sides the Hall is environed with plantations, excluding the prospect, but imparting a rural and sequestered seclusion, in strong contrast with the advancing buildings of the adjacent neighbourhood.

Formerly, the approach from Manchester was through Beswick and Bradford by a narrow and winding lane, since superseded by New road. The fold was four acres in extent, and contained three distinct piles of outhousing, correspondingly large with the size of the farm. The Wheat Barn has been converted into a farm-house, but the steps are still traceable which led into the upper chamber, used as the " garner," or granary. The Oat Barn adjoins the present highway, and, though patched by the insertion of bricks and mortar, was originally erected upon crooks, the foundations being rough ashlar flags, and the superstructure oak timber, covered in with grey slates. The Great Barn, in addition to bays for hay and corn, was, in part, adapted for a shippon. It was a very long and, comparatively, low post and petrel erection, with a thatched roof, remarkably acute in pitch, and extending in dripping eaves considerably beyond the walls. A tradition, quoted by Hollingworth two centuries ago,* and still current, derives the materials of this picturesque structure from the spoliation of Old Saint Mary's, Manchester. The woodwork generally, and especially the oaken principals were beautifully decorated. To use our informant's own words, " Wi' cut un carv'd effigies i'th' Catholic style, o'th' blessed Virgin, saints, angels, un o' mack o'flowers, un had bin part o'th' church ot stoode wheere Saint Ann's-square is neaw." The barn portion became ruinous, and fell down many years ago, and the remainder was accidentally destroyed by fire, September 23, 1852, but, fortunately, a sketch had previously been taken by one of the brethren of the Manchester Rosicrusian Society.

An old domestic chapel, or oratory, stood within the moat, and, it is said, a few paces north-west of the Hall, until its demolition in the early part of last century. The materials, including " large, red rockstones, similar to those in the Old Church steeple," were converted into piggeries and conveniences. The old font is stated to have been transferred to the Collegiate Church, and the four bells (which tradition represents as having been brought from the old parish church on its rebuilding in the fifteenth century) are reputed to have been thus disposed of : one presented to Gorton Chapel ; another to Newton Chapel ; the third sent to the chapel of Smedley Hall, a seat of the Cheethams ; and the fourth retained at Clayton Hall.

However this might have been, the most venerable relic now remaining at the hall is the ancient bell, measuring in depth 12 inches, external circumference 26 inches near the crown, and 51 inches at the mouth, where the internal diameter is 16½ inches. Its general thickness is one inch, except near the mouth, where it increases to 1⅜ inches, and it emits a clear sound. Around the outer edge of the mouth, in old English characters, and probably in Norman-French,

---

* " Chronicles of Manchester," p. 44.

divided by a rose and crown, favourite badges or cognizances, is the motto, or inscription, "Ie [for Je] atende Meleor," meaning, "I expect [or wait for] better [things.]"

It has often been asserted by aged people that some four score years ago, gravestones were remaining in the Chapel yard-meadow, lying to the west of the moat, but no record of interments there have been met with. Indeed from the following abstract of a will, proved at Chester, it is probable that in Queen Elizabeth's time, there were no graveyards attached to either Gorton or Newton Chapel. James Smyth, of Droylsden, servant to Sir John Byron, Knight, by will dated July 19, 1587, directs his "bodie to be buried in ye churchyard of Manchester, as neare to the plane tree as can be."

Clayton Mill, probably once a soke mill for the Byron tenantry of Droylsden, Failsworth, &c., stood locally in Failsworth, being on the north side of the Medlock at Clayton-Bridge. During the tenancy of Joseph Hawthorn, on November 15th, 1757, the structure was destroyed by an infuriated mob, consisting of a large body of men from Ashton, Oldham, Saddleworth, and other places, armed with implements of husbandry and other rustic weapons, who met on Newton Heath, and, visiting the mill, found, as it was alleged, human bones and other offensive matter ready for grinding and admixture with the flour and meal. After wreaking vengeance on the place, destroying both the building and machinery, they proceeded to Manchester, where, in the Market-place, occurred the celebrated "Shude-hill fight" immortalised by "Tim Bobbin."

About a century earlier there seems to have been a rival mill, the site of which is forgotten, for in April, 1648, George Traves, nephew to Humphrey Chetham, headed a large party in "endeavouring to pull up Captain Whitworth's wear belonging to his mill." There had been great throwing of stones, to the hazard of several men's lives. Bulwarks and cabins having been made for the defence of themselves, in the way or manner of war, Mr. Whitworth instituted legal proceedings, which, five years afterwards, were still pending, and the result is yet unknown.

THE BYRONS.

The Byrons, of Clayton and Rochdale, Lancashire, and Newstead Abbey, Notts, are descended from Ralph de Buron, who at the time of the Conquest and of the Doomsday survey, held divers manors in Notts and Derbyshire. Hugo de Buron (living 1143-4), grandson of Ralph, and feudal baron of Horestan, retiring, *temp.* Henry III., from secular affairs, professed himself a monk, and held the hermitage of Kirsale, or Kersall, near Manchester, under the priory of Lenton. His sons were Sir Roger and Hugh de Buron. Robert de Buron [Byron], son of Sir Roger de Buron, in the first King John (1199-1200), married Cecilia, daughter and heiress of Sir Richard Clayton, of Clayton, and thereby obtained the manor and estates of Clayton. Failsworth and the township of Droylsden were soon after added to their Lancashire estates. Their son, Robert de Byron, lord of Clayton, was witness to a grant of Pyling Hay, in this county, to the monks of Cockersand, for the repose of the souls of Henry II. and Richard I. ; and his son, John de Byron, who was seated at Clayton, twenty-eighth Edward I. (1299), was governor of York, and had all his lands in Rochdale with his wife Joan, by gift of her father, Sir Baldwin Teutonicus, or Thies, or de Tyas, who was Conservator of the Peace in Lancashire, tenth Edward I. (1281-2). Her first husband was Sir Robert Holland, secretary of Thomas, Earl of Lancaster. Their son was Sir John de Byron, Knight, lord of Clayton, who was one of the witnesses to the charter granted to the burgesses of Manchester by Thomas Grelle, lord of that manor, in 1301. The two first witnesses to that document were " Sirs John Byron, Richard Byron, Knight." These were father and son. Sir John married Alice, cousin and heir of Robert Banastre, of Hindley, in this county. Their son, Sir Richard, lord of Cadenay and Clifton, had grant of free warren in his demesne lands in Clayton, Butterworth, and Royton, on the 28th of June, 1308 ; he served in Parliament for Lincolnshire, and died before twenty-first Edward

III. (1347-8). His son was Sir James de Byron, who died before twenty-fourth Edward III. (1350-1). His son and heir was Sir John de Byron, who was knighted by Edward III. at the siege of Calais (1346-7), and dying without issue, was succeeded by his brother, Sir Richard, before fourth Richard II. (1380-1). Sir Richard died in 1398, and was succeeded by his son, Sir John *le* Byron, who received knighthood before third Henry V. (1415-16), and was one of the knights of the shire seventh Henry VI. (1428-9). He married Margery, daughter of John Booth, of Barton. His eldest son, Richard le Byron, dying in his father's life-time, and Richard's son, James, dying without issue, the estates passed to Richard's brother, Sir Nicholas, of Clay-ton, who married Alice, daughter of Sir John Boteler, of Beausy, or Bewsy, near Warrington. Their son and heir was Sir John, who was Constable of Nottingham Castle, and Sheriff of Lancashire in 1441 and 1442. Sir John fought in the battle of Bosworth Field, on the side of Henry VII., and was knighted on the field. Dying with-out issue in 1488, he was succeeded by his brother (then thirty), Sir Nicholas, Sheriff of Lancashire in 1459, who was made Knight of the Bath in 1501, and died in January, 1503-4. His son and heir, Sir John Byron, was steward of the manors of Manchester and Rochdale; and on the dissolution of the monasteries, he had a grant of the priory of Newstead, May 28, 1540. From that time, the family made Newstead their principal seat, instead of Clayton. His three eldest sons, Nicholas and two others, dying with-out issue, Sir John was succeeded by his youngest son, Sir John, knighted in 1579. Sir John's eldest son, Sir Nicholas, distinguished himself in the wars in the Low Countries, and at the battle of Edgehill (October 23, 1642). He was Colonel-General of Cheshire and Shropshire. His younger brother, Sir John, was made K.B. at the corona-tion of James I., and a baronet in 1603. Owing to the failure of the elder line, this Sir John became ancestor of the Lords Byron. Sir Nicholas was succeeded by his son, Sir John, who was made K.B. at the coronation of Charles I. He was appointed by that king Lieutenant of the

Tower in 1642, contrary to the wish of Parliament; commanded the body of reserve at Edgehill; and was created Lord Byron of Rochdale, October 24, 1643. In consequence of his devotion to the Royal cause (for he fought against Oliver Cromwell at the battle of Preston, in August, 1648), his manor of Rochdale was sequestered. So great was his lordship's Royalist zeal, that he was one of the seven specially exempted from the clemency of the Government in the Act of Oblivion, passed by Parliament on the execution of Charles I. Dying at Paris, in 1652, without issue, he was succeeded by his cousin Richard (son of Sir John, the baronet just mentioned), who became second Lord Byron, and died October 4, 1679, aged seventy-four. He was succeeded by his eldest son, William, who died November 13, 1695, and was succeeded by his fourth son, William, who died August 8, 1736, and was succeeded by a younger son, William, fifth Lord Byron, who was born in November, 1722, killed William Chaworth in a duel, January, 1765, and died May 19, 1798. He was succeeded by his great nephew, George Gordon, the poet, sixth Lord Byron, who was born January 22, 1788, and died at Missolonghi, Greece, in April, 1824.

THE CHETHAMS, OF CLAYTON.

The reputed manor of Clayton, and Clayton Hall, which had been the chief seat or residence of the Byrons for about 420 years, were purchased by the Chethams from the former family. Sir John Byron, the elder, of Newstead, and Sir John Byron, the younger, Knights, by indenture of February 20, 1620, in consideration of £4,700, convey to George Chetham, of London, grocer, and Humphrey Chetham, of Manchester, chapman, in fee, all that capital messuage called Clayton Hall, together with the demesne lands ; and all that park, or enclosed impaled ground, called Clayton Park ; and all the moss-turbary and soil thereof in Clayton, Failsworth, Manchester, Ashton, Woodhouses, and Droylsden, not formerly sold by Sir John Byron, the son; and all that water corn mill, called Clayton Mill, with all dams, mills, pools, &c.; and all the highways,

lanes, waste grounds, and other ways and passages, and the
ground or soil of the same in Clayton. All the messuages,
tenements, and cottages in Clayton, Failsworth, Droylsden,
Woodhouses, and Manchester, with all closes, fields, &c.,
thereto belonging, in the occupation of Richard Heap, Robert
Hibbert, Widow Hill, Nicholas Johnson, William Clough,
Thomas Taylor, Edmund Asheton, John Travers, and
William Scrimshaw [Grimshaw]. The deed was executed
only by Sir John Byron, jun., and his lady. It appears by
an endorsement, signed George Chetham, that no part of
the soil of the highways in Failsworth, extending from
Newton Heath northward towards Hollinwood, was to pass
the said feoffment.

Henry Chetham, of Crumpsall, had seven sons by his first
wife. James, his eldest surviving son, succeeded to the
Crumpsall estate. Three others, George, Humphrey (the
founder), and Ralph, embarked in the Manchester trade.
George, the second son of Henry, was baptised in May, 1576,
and was buried from Clayton, January 5, 1626-27. This
George was doubtless the joint purchaser of Clayton, with
his more eminent though younger brother, Humphrey,
when they were respectively forty-one and forty years of
age. George is said to have resided at Clayton from the
date of its purchase, when he retired from the business in
London, till his death in 1627, when his brother and
co-partner, Humphrey, the founder, succeeded him at
Clayton, and chiefly resided there till his own death in
1653, altogether about twenty-six years.

By an indenture of November 29, 1635, eight years after
first going thither, Humphrey Chetham leased Clayton
Hall, with the appurtenances, demesne lands, tenements,
gardens, orchards, &c., for ten years, at an annual rent of
£300, to James Jollie, or Jolly, of Droylsden, clothier, who,
as Major Jolly, was afterwards found in possession. But
notwithstanding this lease to another, Humphrey Chetham
did not give up either his entire occupation, tenancy, or
residence, in Clayton Hall, as the reservations in the lease
itself show. The first of these is—"Except and always
reserved, out of the present demise or lease, unto the said

Humphrey Chetham, his heirs and assigns, one little closet
in the dining parlour of and in the said capital messuage,
and the chamber standing or being over the gate-house
thereof." Other reservations are the new stable, the
paddock, part of the demesne, the moss-rooms, and all such
coal pits and mines of coals as are already found, made, and
dug in any part of the fields belonging to the demesne lands
of Clayton. The lessee is to pay all usual taxes, church-
rates, and poor-rates; and the lessor all unaccustomed leys
and charges, amongst which are enumerated,—King's leys
and taxes; the armour, weapons, light-horse, and pikemen
for war, with which the lessor is chargeable; and the yearly
contributions or benevolence paid or given to the minister
for the time being, "as leynes or hyreds" at the chapel of
Gorton. Then come further covenants—"If James Jollie
plow or soweth corn more than fifty acres, he is to pay after
the rate of £5 per acre, over and above the annual rent."
Then—"James Jollie is to have and receive all the boons*
and services which yearly shall arise to be payable, performed, or done by John Gilliam, Richard Heape, and
George Kenion, by force and virtue of the several leases
whereby they enjoy the messuages and lands in their several
occupations."

It is true that during this ten years' lease, no proof is
found of Humphrey's residence at Clayton; but that he
occasionally came there is most probable; and, indeed,
various facts indicate that Clayton Hall was his favourite
residence. He lived much there; his favourite table-chair,
or chair-table, is still shown in one of the rooms, and he
died there September 20, 1653. He dates letters from
"Clayton," in March, 1635, and November, 1648; and one
of the last business letters he ever wrote (during the absence
of his usual amenuensis, who had gone to bury a child)

---

* Roby states that in a MS. of receipts and disbursements,
belonging to the Chethams, kept in the time of Charles II.,
there is an item for money paid for gloves to the boon
shearers at Clayton Hall.—*Traditions of Lancashire*, 1843,
vol. 1, *p.* 176.

bears date—"Claito ye 4 of Maye, 1653." One of his wills,
dated September 13, 1631, began—"I, Humphrey Chetham,
of Clayton, in the county of Lancaster, Esq.;" and his last
will, dated December 16, 1651, commences—"I, Humphrey
Chetham, of Clayton." This will sets forth the settlement
of Clayton, by indenture of December 8, 1651 (just eight
days before the execution of his last will), between himself
and William Langton, Robert Mawdsley, Oswald Mosley,
and John Lomax, by which he conveys to them the manor
house called Clayton Hall, &c., to the use of George
Chetham, son of his brother, James Chetham, and his heirs
male; in default thereof to George Chetham, son of his
brother, Ralph Chetham, and his heirs male, and in default
to his right heirs. He charges Clayton estate with a clear
yearly rent charge of £138, which he devises to the feoffees
for the maintenance of his projected hospital, and he
appointed his nephews, George and Edward Chetham (sons
of his brother James by different mothers), his executors.

Humphrey died at, and was buried from, Clayton Hall,
his funeral being a most costly one, amongst the items
being £111 paid to Mr. Minshull, for "switte meats and
imbalming the body," and the aggregate cost being £1,161
19s. 6d. His senior nephew and heir, George, eldest son
of James (the founder's eldest brother), was the next owner
and occupant of Clayton Hall. It is stated that he was
born on July 1, 1594, and died December 13, 1664, aged
seventy years. He married Elizabeth, daughter of Henry
Johnson, of Manchester, mercer, and had several children.
He for some time resided in London, where he was sheriff
and alderman, and was high sheriff of Lancashire in
1659-60. In 1655, he was by far the largest ratepayer in
Droylsden. On the 1st of December, in the year preceding,
he had been nominated a feoffee of Manchester Free Grammar School; and on the 26th of February, 1661, he was
reappointed. He was entitled Lord of Turton, Clayton,
&c. One of his account books was entitled "A Cash Book
of George Chetham, Esq., of Turton and Clayton, from
1633 to 1637," and another is dated "from 1640 to 1670";
but this last year was six years after his decease. His

monument in St. Mary's Chantry, Manchester Cathedral, is inscribed "Georgius Chetham, de Turton et *Clayton*, armiger."

Connected with Clayton must briefly be noticed another George Chetham, cousin of this George, the eldest son of Ralph (youngest brother of the founder), who was born May 1, 1623, and a legatee for £200 in his uncle Humphrey's will. In Cooper's MSS., it is stated that he was "crazy, hippish, and much dejected." He lived at Clayton Hall; but being "sore afraid" [was this of Clayton Hall boggart?] he was brought to Leer (Lever), near Turton, and lived with Mr. Crompton, and died a bachelor. He was commonly called "Mad Chetham"; and it is said that, once holding a glass of wine in his hand, and letting it fall, he exclaimed, "Thus fell Turton and Clayton!"

To return to the Clayton estate as bequeathed and charged by the founder's will. Although neither of his executors was able to fulfil the requests of the founder in converting sums of money and two rent charges into lands and tenements for the maintenance of the hospital, this was done by James (George's son) purchasing the Sutton estate in 1676; and Samuel (the son of this last James, and grandson of George the executor) in 1700 conveyed the manor and lordship of Sutton, and other lands in Derbyshire, to the feoffees for ever, and thus discharged the estates of Clayton and Turton of their respective rent charges. This Samuel died without issue on March 20, 1774-5, in his sixty-ninth year; and his monumental inscription in St. Mary's Chantry describes him as of "Castleton, Turton, *Clayton*," &c. His estates descended to his only surviving brother, Humphrey, who married, but died without issue in July, 1749, and the estates then descended to his second cousin, Edward Chetham, barrister, who died unmarried in February, 1769, in his eightieth year, when his estates were divided between his sisters Alice (who had married Adam Bland) and Mary (wife of Samuel Clowes) by a partition deed, dated October 31, 1770. By this deed the Broughton and Kersal property went to Mrs. Clowes; the Clayton and Turton property to Mrs. Bland. Mrs. Bland's only child married at

the Collegiate Church a Spanish merchant, named Mordecai
Greene, who thus received the Clayton estates with his
wife. Their sole issue was James Greene, of Turton and
Clayton Hall, who married Miss Ann Brigstock, and having
served in Parliament for the borough of Arundel, and held
many diplomatic situations on the Continent, died in 1814,
leaving five daughters and co-heiresses—viz., Mary Ann,
wife of Edward Frere, Esq.; Arabella Penelope Eliza, wife
of Peter Richard Hoare, Esq.; Charlotte Alice, wife of
Edward William Seymour, Esq.; Angelina Francis, wife
of George Matthew Hoare, Esq.; and Anna Sophia. P. R.
Hoare, Esq., is now the owner of the ancient manor, manor
house, and estates of Clayton, the possession of which has
been traced from the first year of the reign of King John
to the present time, a period extending over six centuries
and a half.

John Wallworth resided at Clayton Hall in the middle of
the seventeenth century, and the register of Gorton Chapel
records the baptism of two of his children in 1656 and in
1661 as taking place in "Cleeton Hoole." Richard Entwistle, of Clayton, was buried at Gorton in April, 1671;
and John, son of James Neeld, of Clayton Hall, was baptised in December, 1697, at the same place. Thomas Whitaker, of Clayton, in April, 1723, was a warden of Newton
Chapel, where, in October, 1728, was interred John Edge,
of "Cleton Hall." Mr. Edmund Newton, the next recorded
occupant, was an agent of the Chethams. His wife's name
was Esther; and in March, 1744, their son Richard was
baptised at Gorton. He buried a son, Joseph, at Newton,
in December, 1747, and continued to reside at the Hall until
the close of 1772, when he was followed by John Wood,
who farmed the estate about twelve years. At this period
the Hall was the only dwelling on the estate. Coming into
the possession of the Thornleys, of Audenshaw, Thomas
Roberts farmed it nine years—first for them on commission,
and afterwards on his own account. Samuel Howard
followed in 1803, and was succeeded by Benjamin Wors-
wick, about 1823, who farmed for the co-heirs. He built
the "Humphrey Chetham" public-house, and some cot-

tages at West End, and, failing, afterwards emigrated to America.

Scanty information precludes a chapter devoted to heraldry and genealogy. Crests and armorial bearings have been borne or claimed by the families of Clayton, Byron, Greene, Hoare, Christy, Ashworth, Hadwen, Lees, Wood, Chadwick, &c. The pedigree of the Byrons, previously recorded, is the only detailed attempt at tracing family lineage and descent.

From remote times Droylsden seems to have been divided into separate tenements, or estates, comprising some thirty to forty farms, and having in addition a few cottage dwellings. In the reign of James I., after an uninterrupted enjoyment of more than four centuries, the estates of the township passed by sale and subdivision from the Byrons into the possession of numerous small landed proprietors; thus, as a rule, each farm, after this period, constituted the freehold of its resident, sturdy and substantial yeoman; but gradually most of these inheritances, either by sale, distaff, or bequest, became alienated from the families of the original owners.

Amongst the most ancient landed proprietors in the township must be included Sir John de Asheton, of Ashton-under-Lyne, although at present the representative of the family owns only two small closes at Moorside, about four acres in extent, and acquired, it is said, by bequest from a family steward about a century ago. It appears from the celebrated "rent roll," compiled in 1422, by Sir John Asheton, that John the Byron, Knight, paid for Whitworth lands, in Droylsden, the yearly rent of xx*d.*, during the lives of Richard Unton, and Alys his wife, and also the same "John Buron" paid xvi*s.* annually for a parcel of the Moss.

In the twenty-first Henry VII. (1505-6), John Ellawre (Ellor) appears as plaintiff, and Ralph Holland as defendant, in a disputed title to lands in Openshaw, Drilesden Moor, Wrang, and Opensha.

John Booth, of Chetham, yeoman, in 1617, purchased from the Byrons, for £240, the farm house and the two further fields, barnfield, further and nearer moorfields, yarncroft, and little moorcroft, the orchard at the back of the barn, and the orchard at the new bay, which now constitute the estate appertaining to Edge Lane Mills. In the year following, Booth purchases from Ralph Buredsell, of Droylesden, yeoman, for £4 15s., a certain moss doal in Droylesden; and a few weeks afterwards disposes of both, at a profit of £20, to Edward Walklate, yeoman, of Ludworth, in Derbyshire. Walklate, some three years afterwards, married Anne Bearde, and settled the estate on their issue. In 1655, it was, apparently, in the possession of Ralph and Thomas Walklate. In 1697, William Walklate, of Ludworth, yeoman, only son and heir of Ralph Walklate, deceased, who was brother and heir of Edward Walklate, of the same place, deceased, sells the estate and a small one adjoining, for £460, to Ralph Pycroft, of Manchester, chapman, who by will, dated November, 1698, leaves it to his grandson, Ralph Nicholson. In 1717, Ralph Nicholson, of Bolton, linen draper, sold the original estate of thirteen acres for £321 10s. to James Grimshaw, chapman, in whose family it continued more than a century.

Ann Wodd (Wood), in 1614, purchased from the Byrons, for £10, the messuage and close called the Croft that the house standeth in (now the site of the Recreation Grounds), and two moss doals in Droylsden Moss, or Moor.

George Birch, Esq., of Birch, held lands and messuages in Droylesden, as appears by his inquisition post mortem, September 9, 1613, which lands, in 1655, were in the tenancy of Ralph Hibbert, jun. Thomas Birch, Esq., of Higher Ardwick, by will, dated January 3, 1746, leaves his lands in Droylsden, then in the occupation of John Redfern, to his brother, George Birch, and his heirs and assigns for ever.

George Blomely, as is set forth in his inq. p. m., sixteenth Charles I. (1640-1), died seized of land and messuages in Droylsdale.

The Halls were a respectable yeomanry family, long resident at the (South) Clockhouse, which was so named early in the seventeenth century. James Hall, of Droylsden, gentleman, on September 9, 1613, is found acting on the inquisition post mortem of George Birch, Esq., of Birch Hall. According to a note in the "Life of Adam Martindale," published by the Chetham Society, he seems to have been an agent of the Byrons, and was living September 18, twelfth James (1614), but died shortly afterwards. Martindale, who married his second daughter, Elizabeth, in December, 1646, describes his father-in-law as "a freeholder of good ranke," and, by report, a most eminent Christian, but dead long before. Certain freehold lands in Droylsden, Droylesden, or Drylsden, and now a part of the Clockhouse farm, were conveyed in 1614-15 by Sir John Byron, of Newstead, and Sir John Byron, the younger, of Royton, near Oldham, to William Buerdsell; and the same gentleman, on October 22, 1617, in consideration of £180, also conveyed another portion of the present estate, then in the tenancy of John Hall and Cicely Hall, widow, to Richard Holland, of Denton, and his assigns for ever. Cicely Hall was relict of the above James Hall. She afterwards married James Jollie, and survived to a very great age.

James Hall and John Hall, sons of James Hall, of Drielsden, yeomen, are mentioned as "his beloved kinsmen" in the will of Edward Shacklock, of Moston, dated October, 1618, and printed in Booker's "History of Blackley." John Hall owned the estate, November 14, 1639, by purchase from the Hollands. James Hall was a Droylsden ratepayer in 1655. John Hall, of the Clockhouse, buried a son, John, at Gorton Chapel in July, 1700; and in March, 1712, disposed of the estate to Mr. Miles Nield, merchant and chapman, of Manchester. This farm, and other property in Droylsden, came into the possession of William Clowes, merchant, of Manchester, in February, 1738, on his marriage with Elizabeth, one of the two daughters and co-heiresses of the above Miles Nield. John Peploe Birch, Esq., only son and heir of the Rev. Samuel Peploe, Doctor of Law, and Chancellor of the diocese of Chester, became possessed of the Droylsden property in 1764, by marriage with Ann, only child of the above William and Elizabeth Clowes, in whose possession the Clockhouse estate remained until May 2, 1801, when they sold it to Messrs. Robert Bagnall and William Robinson, of Manchester. These gentlemen pulled down the ancient mansion, a rather extensive post and petrel erection, with a westerly aspect, and built two modern dwellings some forty yards west northwest of the former site. By a diagonal line they divided the estates into two portions, which, after passing through several hands, are now jointly the property of Edmund Buckley, Esq., of Higher Ardwick.

The Halls for a century and a half worshipped and baptised at Gorton Chapel, and interred there for a century; and they had also a seat, or pew, in Newton Chapel. John Hall, sen., of the Clockhouse, was buried at Gorton, in February, 1740; and lastly, Mr. John Hall, of Droylsden, whitster, in October, 1757. The family terminated in females, one of whom, Ann, married William Hulton, Esq., of Hulton Park, whom she survived, dying in 1802.

The earliest memorials of the interesting family of Jolly begin with 1635, when James Jollie, or Jolly, took a lease of Clayton Hall. When the Lancashire Presbyterical Classes were instituted, October 2, 1646, James Jolly, of Droylsden, yeoman, was constituted a lay member of the same. He married Cicely, widow of John Hall, who survived him, and was still living in 1688, aged ninety-one, when Newcome records her as sending to him to pray a deal for her.

Entering the service of the Parliament, Jollie became a captain, then major, and lastly held the obnoxious office of provost-marshal in the Parliamentary army in the county of Lancaster. His name appears amongst the ratepayers in 1655, and he died eleven years afterwards, leaving three sons, all of whom had been brought up in the university. The most famous was Thomas, of Trinity College, Cambridge, born in 1629, the Independent minister of Altham, in Lancashire, in 1649, and from whence he was ejected by the Act of Uniformity. Subsequently he built a place of

worship on part of his own estate, at Wymondhouses, near
Clitheroe, where he continued to officiate till his death,
which took place April 16, 1703. Matthew Henry speaks
of him, says Calamy ("Nonconformists' Memorial"), as a
minister of the first rank for gifts and graces. Slate, in his
" Select Nonconformists' Remains," gives an interesting
biographical sketch of him. His son Timothy was minister
of the Nonconformists of Sheffield, where he was ordained
in 1681, and died in 1714, leaving a son, Timothy, who died
in 1757, aged sixty-five, having been for thirty-one years a
pastor in London.

John, son of Major Jollie, of Trinity College, Dublin, an
admirer of Scotch Presbyterianism, was ejected from Nor-
bury, Cheshire, in 1662, and afterwards resided and preached
in Gorton, where he died suddenly, June 17, 1682. He
was little more than forty years of age, and left behind him
several children, one of whom succeeded him in the ministry.
Calamy describes him as a man of fertile genius and resolute
spirit, and remarkably spiritually minded. Of Nathan, the
third son, it is recorded that in after life he resided in
Chester.

It seems that the township did form the residence of one
gentleman in 1665, for on March 11 in that year, Mr. James
Wallwork, of Droylsden, was required to appear at Manchester, before Norroy, King of Arms, in order to register
his ancestry, coat of arms, &c.

Droylsden does not seem to have enjoyed the dignity of
conferring a family surname,—a circumstance somewhat
unusual for a Lancashire township, but probably arising
from the Clayton and Byron families having, in succession,
owned all the lands of the township to the exclusion of
other landowners and yeomen. Still, a John Drysdale is
alluded to in the "Shuttleworth Accounts," published by
the Chetham Society.

As showing the family nomenclature of the period, the
list of ratepayers in 1655 is not without interest. Arranged
alphabetically they were as follows :—Edward Ashton and
his son; William Beardsall; James Bexwicke; Edward
Boardman; John Brooke; Thomas Byron; Geo. Cheetham,

Esq.; Robert Glossop; Widow Gorton; Widow Gorton, the younger; George Grimshaw; Widow Grimshaw and her son; George Hall; James Hall; Richard Heape; Ralph Hibbert, of the Fields; Ralph Hibbert, of the Moss; Ralph Hibbert, the younger, of Birchlands; Robert Hilton; Mr. Samuel Jenkinson; James Jollie; Widow Kenion; Widow Kenion, the younger; Robert Leech; Joseph Ouldham; Mary Parr; James Tailor; John Thorp; Thomas Thorp; Ralph Walkelate; Thomas Walkelate; and William Wood.

Robert Walker, of Smallshawe, gentleman, and William Walker, his son and heir apparent, in consideration of £39, convey to Nicholas Hodgkinson, of Droylesden, bricklayer, all that messuage, tenement, and the great and little crofts situate in Droylesden, Drylsden, or Droylsden, and now known as Little Droylsden, and also freedom of turbary on a moss room, which is part of Droylesden Moss or Moor, as agreed upon by Sir John Byron, knight, deceased, and Marie Hunt, deceased, to be the moss room belonging to the above tenement, containing five yards in breadth, and extending from the end or side of a close in Droylesden, late in the tenure of Robert Graves, deceased, and in length as far as the turbary extends southerly. The conveyance is dated April 9, fifteenth Charles II. (*i.e.* 1663, as in legal instruments his reign was reckoned to begin at the death of his father), being signed by the Walkers and witnessed by Thomas Strangways and James Hodgkinson. The estate passed to Mary, only surviving child of Hodgkinson, and wife of John Herron, of Droylsden, weaver; then to her eldest son and heir, John Herron, of the same place, farmer, who died intestate; next to hisonly child, Mary, who married a Wilde, survived him, and in 1758, sold the estate for £100 to James Walker, of Manchester, thread throwster. Thence it descended to his son and heir, William Walker, of Hollinwood, husbandman, who sold the same in 1772, to John Pott, of Droyslden, whitster; and it is now vested in William Howarth, of Newton Heath.

The will of a Baguley, of Failsworth, about 1554, occurs in the Lanc. MSS., and from another document it appears that on October 10, 1614, Sir John Byron, senior, and Sir John

Byron, junior, convey to Adam Bagguley, yeoman, all that messuage and tenement in Failsworth and Droylsden, then in his occupation, and all these closes, viz. the Yarn Croft, the Summer Hey, with the green lane adjoining, the Suid (Shude) Hill, the Middle Hey, the Highest Eye, the Pingot, the Wheat Eye, the Greenfield Clough, the Barrickfield, the Calf Croft, and part of the Barrackfield Clough : purchase money, £180. A settlement of these lands was made November 14, 1640, upon the marriage of Adam Baguley, junior, with Elizabeth, daughter of Thomas Pyecroft, of Droylsden, yeoman.

George and Humphrey Chetham, chapmen, lease to John Hewett, May 21, 1625, a messuage and tenement in Droylsden, for three lives at an annual rent of £12 13s. 4d.

The first person of the name of Walker alluded to as resident in Droylsden is Charles Walker, in 1580, mentioned in Booker's "History of Denton." After the lapse of fifty years occurs Jane, daughter of Charles Walker de Droylsden, who fell off a bridge, was drowned, and was buried at Ashton Parish Church, in July, 1630. Apparently towards the close of the seventeenth century, the only person of opulence in the township was William Walker, as his name alone from Droylsden occurs in the MS. parchment roll of a "List of names of all persons in the hundred of Salford chargeable to the subsidy of King James II." In 1758, the Droylsden butcher was named James Walker.

The antique farm house at Greenside, now occupied by Mr. Gibson, was erected, as appears by an inscription (J. G. and M. G., 1660), by John and Mary Guilliam, or Gilliam. The following particulars are derived from "Notitia Cestriensis," ii. 91-2. John Gilliam, of Levenshulme, gent., was son and heir of John Gilliam, of the same place, esq. (a captain in the Parliamentary army, and justice of the peace), and his wife, Mary, daughter of James Halliwell, of Pikehouse, in the parish of Rochdale, gent. John Gilliam, jun., was baptised at Littleborough, July 2, 1658, and married Jane, daughter of Thomas Percival, of Royton, gent. By will dated June 18, 1688, and proved at Chester,

October 26, in the same year, he left many legacies for charitable purposes, and settled his very large estates in Droylsden, and many other places, on his only child, Jane Gilliam, who subsequently married John Greaves, Esq., of Manchester, high sheriff of Lancashire, in 1783, leaving a son, Edward, who died in 1824. The property is now vested in two nephews.

Several old families bore the name of Grimshaw, and in order to distinguish them, one is said to have varied the form to Grunshaw, or Grunsho. The Yew Tree farm has been the inheritance of one of these families for nearly two centuries and a half.

From Booker's "Blackley," it appears that John Diggles, of Manchester, linen draper, and of Booth Hall, Blackley, by will dated August 7, 1719, gives to his son James his messuages and tenements situate in Droylsden, &c. John Diggles, of Booth Hall, Blackley, but now of Brompton-row, Middlesex, by will dated November 11, 1781, bequeaths to Thomas Bayley all his messuages, farms, &c., in Droylsden and other places.

Joseph Yates, of Manchester, gent., died in 1705, leaving a son, Joseph Yates, Esq., a Droylsden ratepayer in 1731-2. His son, Sir Joseph Yates, Knight, was some time one of the judges of the Court of King's Bench, and was transferred thence to the Common Pleas, which event he survived little more than a month, dying June 7, 1770, aged forty-eight. His death is recorded in the "Gentleman's Magazine," without any further ostentation than the remark that he was "One of the honestest of judges that ever filled the bench."

Samuel Sandiford, of Droylsden, linen webster, in May, 1726, for £200, conveys to Thomas Higginbotham, of Mottram-in-Longdendale, one dwelling house and the four acres, two acres, and the meadow containing eight acres, heretofore in the occupation of John Lees, of Droylsden, husbandmen, deceased, and since of his relict, Martha Lees, and now of the above Samuel Sandiford. A part of this estate forms the site of Droylsden Mills. By will dated August 5, 1775, Thomas Higinbotham, of Mottram, grocer,

bequeaths his freehold estate in Droylsden, in the occupation of Thomas Herod, to his nephew, Thomas Middleton,
of Chapel-en-le-Frith, grocer, subject to an annuity of £5,
to his nephew William (brother to Thomas) Middleton, and
a like annuity to his cousin Arminal Middleton. Some
eight years afterwards, Thomas Middleton mortgaged the
estate for £300 to a Miss Appleton, and within memory the
ownership fell into abeyance. It is now the property of
Edmund Buckley, Esq., of Higher Ardwick.

DOMESTIC ARCHITECTURE.

The early huts, cots, or domiciles of the peasantry were
slight structures of one storey, open to the rafters, and
divided into "house part" and dormitory. These primitive
erections consisted of a vertical framework of oaken crooks
inserted in the earth, and pegged well together. The lower
portion was crossed with transverse timbers, and the inter-
stices were filled in with laths, wattles, or wicker work,
and plastered with clay, in the style locally designated
"raddle and daub." The upper or roof part of the skeleton,
was hipped at both ends, thatched with straw, and usually
curved like a swine's back. If not adorned with an entrance
porch, perforated with an eyelet hole, there was generally,
in lieu thereof, a wooden speer to keep the draught from
the hearth. The door was kept closed, or shut, with the aid
of a sneck, or catch, and was opened or unlatched by means
of the finger-hole, or else by the "sneck bant" and handle.
No preliminary "knocking at the door" was then needed.
Bells, knockers, and spring locks were undreamt of; and
visitors, whether friends or foes, rich men or beggars, let
themselves in. and, if at meal time, were bade to make
themselves free, and assured that they were welcome to
what the house could afford.

The floors were commonly at a lower level than the
surrounding soil, and were formed simply of earth or clay,
trodden firm by the feet-patterings of successive generations.
The light of heaven could only stealthily penetrate through
a casement window or two, glazed with small lozenge panes
of a greenish hue. If the house had two storeys, the

attic was honoured, also, with a little dormer window, or solar gable, which, starting up in the middle, broke the external uniformity of the roof, and imparted thereto quite a picturesque appearance.

There were no attempts at ventilation, and it remains a moot point whether a hole in the thatch, caused by the wear and tear of the elements, did more evil, as a passage for the wet, than good, as a channel for the ingress of fresh air.

Though fast disappearing before the rapid strides of "modern improvement," a few dwellings, slightly altered, yet linger by the borders of the lanes at Greenside and Castle, constituting the only remaining links connecting the Droylsden of the days of great Queen Bess, with that of the days of good Queen Victoria.

Of the superior or yeomanry type of the style, the (South) Clockhouse was a good example; and the rear of a Greenside farm house, now occupied by Mrs. Wood, exhibits some fair specimens of quatrefoiling in post and petrel. These granges, in addition to the dining room and the kitchen, or "house place," as it was emphatically designated, boasted a better room, dignified as "the parlour," and reserved for the best furniture, and used only on festive occasions.

Owing to the increasing scarcity of native timber, that class of buildings, which, with slight modifications, had been current for long centuries, became gradually succeeded by brick edifices about the period of the Restoration. The farm house, at Greenside, occupied by Mr. Gibson, with its spacious and partially wainscotted apartments, lozenge chimney shafts, and other characteristics of the period, is a tolerably good specimen of the semi-manorial dwelling of the latter part of the seventeenth century, and the following description of another is attempted.

Droylsden possesses two out of the five clockhouses met with in Lancashire. The name was apparently derived from possessing horologes,* when those articles were of

---

* *Cloch* is also Norman French for a bell, and the (North) Clockhouse had formerly a bell to ring the farm servants to dinner; the (South) Clockhouse was destitute of a bell, but boasted a large turret clock in the outbuildings.

great rarity and luxury; and to these favoured places no doubt the neighbouring farmers, destitute of accurate time-keepers, would despatch their servants or children to inquire "what o'clock it was." The clockhouse near Clayton-Bridge, is an old house, of mixed stone and brick, erected on an eminence, and approached by a steep path. In the present rear is the old porch, which has been bricked up, and a small window put out where the porch door formerly existed. The porch, which is still open interiorly, contains two old wooden side seats, where it was customary to sit in fine weather. The "house part" differs from ordinary houses in having been panelled in oak. The remains exist on one side wall only. In this wall are two doors; the space between them, eight feet, is panelled to a height of six feet or more, divided by a sort of finial every four feet. Painted upon a plaster panel, midway between the doors, at a good height, are the royal arms of England, as borne by Charles I. and II., surrounded by the garter, but without supporters, exactly as figured in Gwyllim's "Display of Heraldry," p. 439. Beneath are the motto and date, "DIEV ET MON DROIT. 1689." This year was the first of the reign of William and Mary.

The dwelling houses in Fairfield, at the time of erection, were a decided advance in the beauty, usefulness, and comfort of local domestic architecture.

A few modern mansions claim passing attention, and most prominently so Alderdale Lodge, the seat of Abel Buckley, Esq., J.P., which is partly enclosed in gardens, shrubberies, and thriving plantations. The situation is delightful, on the verge of a green knolly meadow, over-looking the vale of the Medlock. North-road, Clayton, is tolerably secluded from the hum and bustle of manufactur-ing life, and bids fair to become the "West End" of Droylsden, containing already several pleasing villas, in the cottage ornée style. The residence of Richard Christy, Esq., with its gabled entrance porch, hip-knobs, clustered chimneys, and bay windows (mullioned and transomed), is worth notice. A number of pretty mansions have sprung up near the south-east verge of the township, but they are locally situated in Audenshaw. Notwithstanding the presence of sand and clay, which is cheaply and expeditiously manufactured into bricks, there has been felt, till lately, a want of an intermediate class of dwellings.

SOCIAL CONDITION, HABITS, CHARACTERISTICS, ETC.

At a time when Droylsden was an obscure village, and, beyond its own borders, a *terra incognito*, the attachment of the few indigenous families to their own kith and kin was remarkably strong. Hence, when wiving, they seldom passed over the claims of their neighbours' daughters in favour of strangers; and consequently, from the intricacies of intermarriage, some century ago, the inhabitants had become a colony of relations, as Byron says—

> " Marrying their cousins— nay, their aunts and nieces,
> Which always spoils the breed, if it increases."

There must have been a reaction of late, as in May, 1851, a Droylsdenian attempted to sell his wife in Stockport market-place,—a fellow weaver at Droylsden Mills starting the bidding at seven pence, which was soon advanced upon up to ten shillings ; but the police dispersed the competitors ere she was " knocked down."

As "little things are great to little men," and inferior commodities are prizeable in a dearth, so, in the absence of more weighty affairs, the gossip of last century chiefly concerned marriages, christenings, and burials, with occasional inquests; also the feats of renowned mowers and reapers— the death of a cow by murrain or milk fever—the state of the few trades struggling in the district—and, too frequently, political and religious animosities — furnished themes for a converse or motives for a fight.

Gipsies periodically bivouacked in the quiet green lanes and " out-o'-way places," and often succeeded in wheedling or purloining something from the villagers; for when their professional dips into futurity and persuasive eloquence elicited scant remuneration, if opportunity presented itself, they were not loth to seize anything which was not either " too hot or too heavy" to remove. At length news of their location reached the town's authorities, when forth marched, staves in hand, the worthy constables and other village officials, and peremptorily " warned them off." This usually effected a strike of their camp, and consequently transferred the attentions of these wandering vagrants to some other and perhaps distant locality.

In the era when the hand loom reigned supreme, owing to the scarcity of lime, cottages were only whitewashed septennially; yet, says an octogenarian, the bedding was not infested with anything worse than fleas. It was then customary for the thrifty housewife, on Monday afternoon, to discard the shuttle for the wash-tub; and on Saturday at noon she knocked off her loom, and then mopped and red sanded the floor, which cleansing lasted till Saturday came round again.

Of course the scale of cottage comforts, in substantiality, if not luxury, of food, improved articles of dress, neatness of dwelling house exteriors, as well as internal conveniences, have increased proportionably with the progress of manufactures, and the number of schools and places of public worship testifies that the social and intellectual and the moral and religious status of the people has been steadily advancing.

One phase of the improved condition of the working classes is exemplified by the fact that, within recollection, say nearly four score years ago, men, even on the Sabbath, were dressed up in fustian. Then arose the innovation of black cloth breeches, which, with the red "senglit," or vest, and the stereotyped fustian jacket, once constituted the tip top of fashion of the Droylsden dandy. Next the beaux of the village introduced blue cloth trousers, figured vests, and blue cloth coats, with brass buttons; and now suits of good broad cloth are worn by every working man on the Sabbath, and by many on the previous afternoon.

In consequence of the cheapness of cotton prints, no Droylsden belle would now think of enrobing herself, either for love or labour, in the once universal and economical " bedgown." Commercial competition and good wages have wholly democratised dress; and now, on the score of

D

finery, it is often difficult to distinguish the mistress from her maid, or the female operative from the millowner's wife.

Coarse kinds of food, of which oatmeal, either as cakes, jannock, or porridge, formed the staple commodity, sufficed the hardy and jocose Droylsdenians of the middle of the last century. Then one butcher satisfied the requirements of the villagers; now it requires sixteen cow, and three calf butchers, in addition to a manufactory for pie meat and stuffing for sausages.

Passing on towards the close of the century, "butty brews," or joining at the expense of manufacture and in the consumption of ales, were notoriously common. Card players were regaled with the contents of a barrel tapped for the occasion; and, if only an odd house was erected, the owner invited his neighbours to the "rearing," as did also fresh tenants to their "house warmings," in order to partake of what, as to quantity, was often miscalled "a sope of drink."

At that period the whole township, perhaps, could not boast half a dozen iron ovens, but brick ones and backstones were common, both in farm house and cottage. Brick ovens, though seldom used, were always brought into requisition for baking a family pie, or roasting a joint of meat in a dripping tin, at the wakes, at Christmas, and other red-letter days. A shop bake house was established on the erection of Fairfield, and, being the only one in the country-side, it was customary to carry out the bread with horse and panniers, through Ashton to Oldham, and even as far as Lees and Saddleworth. Three or four shops were amply sufficient to supply the requirements of Droylsden and its vicinity. John Slater, of Dukinfield, removed to Fairfield in 1786, and under his management the drapery and provision store was for many years the principal shop of its kind in the district. The following also were considered extensive dealers in provisions, viz. :—Robert Booth, near the White Hart; Betty Nicholson, alias Pepper Betty, in Far-lane; and a little later on, Hannah Etchells, near Lane End.

The dietetic economy of a Droylsden family of that period

is thus stated. The custom was for the good wife to bake three pecks of oat cakes per week, the entire family being restricted, except on Sundays, from loaf bread and tea; the matron, alone, might, if she chose, partake daily of the new fangled infusion. The husband breakfasted on "thick porridge and ale dip, with bread and cheese afterwards to fill up the corners." The children had meal porridge and milk, with a luncheon of oat cake and butter, or cheese. Dinner was taken about eleven or twelve, and consisted of dumplings, potato pie, or boiled meat and broth. "Bagging" consisted of oat cake and cheese, or butter, sweet or churned milk and bread, or cheese and bread. Supper was generally much the same as breakfast, but varied occasionally with a rasher of meat or a collop of bacon and potatoes. Other variations or courses were: frumenty, made of wheat boiled in milk; brewis, or oat cake toasted, broken small, and soaked in water wherein a "black pudding" had been boiled, and then seasoned with butter, pepper, and salt, and lastly eaten to the pudding aforesaid; and crab verjuice was eaten with zest by the hungry peasantry. Skim milk could be obtained at 3d. per burn can full, and fresh butter was uncommonly dear when raised to 7d. or 8d. per pound. Although cans and mess pots were in general use, yet ordinarily the whole family, in eating porridge, brewis, &c., dipped their spoons into the same dish.

It is handed down how a Greenside dame, receiving a present of a pound of tea, by the advice of her neighbours, proceeded to treat it like cabbage. After the usual boiling, seasoning, and flavouring, she placed the leaves before her husband, when he returned from labour at night. In vain the good man tried to eat and to like it; and at last, disgusted at the epicurean taste of the day, ordered the new fangled stuff to be pitched into the midden.

As a proof of the primitive simplicity of the inhabitants some four score years ago, it used to be related how, one dark winter's evening, the occupants of the straggling dwellings dotting the margin of Droylsden - lane were frightened out of their wits by the appearance of a "feighery dragon flyin' op th' lone." At length, numbers giving

courage or curiosity, out to the battle rushed the farmers
and their servants with forks and pikels, hatters with their
"stricka pegs," and weavers with their heating irons.
After a long and arduous chase, one of the weavers, more
courageous, or swifter footed than the rest, with a blow of
his searing instrument, succeeded in extinguishing one of its
"two big sheignin' een," and shouted in ecstasy, "Aw've
blinkt it—Aw've blinkt it!" Judge of his chagrin when
requested to pay for one of the night lamps attached to a
gentleman's carriage!

Years afterwards, one evening, an itinerating musician,
from Manchester, entered the White Hart, and found some
hatters and weavers disputing relative to feats in hunting.
" Gentlemen, shall I give you a tune on the *violin?*"
"What does th' chap say, Tum?" "Aw dun kneaw; dost
theau, Bill?" "Neaw, aw conno tell os aw do; bur let's
have o tune ot ony rate." Brim full of intense curiosity,
they cluster round whilst the artist proceeds to untie the
strings of a green, oblong, and mysterious looking bag.
After a penetrative glance, one of the disappointed-sons of
Nimrod roars out in a passion, "Whoy, dang it, it's nowt
bur un arrant fiddle!"

In another instance, two philosophical youths ripped open
a pair of bellows for the purpose of discovering the source
of the wind. A well known farmer ascended a tree, seated
himself on a bough which he intended to lop off, and of
course both fell together in the ditch below.   And, did
space allow, many mischievous but ingenious frolics, and
witty but frivolous diversions, could be enumerated, which
the introduction of Cotton Mills and the New Police, com-
bined with a spreading thirst for intellectual enjoyments,
have for ever put an end to.

RECREATION AND AMUSEMENT.

No account of the May pole has survived in Droylsden,
notwithstanding the past existence of several village greens.
The monotony of the hand loom or baisin was occasionally
relieved by the arrival of a travelling raree show, or a visit
from the mountebanks or other itinerating sons of Thespis.

Practical jokes were keenly relished, and many rural sports engaged in, which have since grown extinct. As the year wheeled round, each season or festival presented its appropriate pastime. Winter brought its slides and football, shinty and trapbad, pole jumping and craddies, hornyholes, trust, hammer and block, foot and a half, prison bars, &c.; Shrove Tuesday its pancakes and "stanging"; and Easter was heralded by pace eggers, and mummers in masks and grotesque attire, singing quaint ditties, reciting chivalrous pieces, or acting the combat of St. George of England with the Turk, and the latter's miraculous restoration by the far travelled doctor. Then came the wake, with its exciting bull baits and more harmless festivities, and gunpowder plot with its toffy and tharcake. Bonfires were kindled under the Round Oak, near Graver-lane, on Lanehead Green, and at Green-lane End. For this purpose the village youngsters industriously scoured the fields for gate posts, decayed trees, and the like, or visited the houses and importuned the inmates for fuel, with this whimsical, doggerel petition—

> " Gunpowder plot shall never be forgot,
> Whilst Old England stands on a rock :
> Up a ladder and down a wall,
> A cob of coal 'll serve us all."

And so Christmas and New Year's tide came apace, and many were the rejoicings thereat. Amongst ancient custon s not quite extinct, having been twice or thrice celebrated in the last half dozen years, is the ceremony of " riding stang," or effigy bearing, when persons have proved faithless to their nuptial vows.

A reaction ensued, intellectual activity set in, and tea meetings, soirées, concerts, lectures, and discussions well nigh quenched athletic exercises and outdoor enjoyments. Whitsuntide trips, and the bowling green at Green's Arms, alone remained ; and many industrious youths truly alleged that, after a hard day's toil, they felt little zest for spending evening after evening in such sedentary recreation as intellectual studies could only afford. To remedy the discontinuance of open air amusements, two steps in the right direction were taken about the same time. The Public

Recreation Grounds, planned for a variety of interesting and invigorating gymnastic exploits calculated to strengthen the youthful frame, were opened with much *éclat*—a procession and tea party forming part of the proceedings—on February 14, 1857. The site was leased for three years, by ten trustees, each of the five religious bodies in the village having two representatives, and their lease will expire in January next. It is lamentable to add that, though much resorted to by the youth of the neighbourhood, this worthy institution languishes for want of pecuniary support.

The manly game of cricket has taken deep root in the locality. The Droylsden Albert Cricket Club, formed 26th August, 1857, leases a field, well adapted for the sport, and furnished with flag poles, and a wooden cot, divided into several compartments. This institution, in a moral point of view, promises to prove beneficial to the neighbourhood, from the intercourse and admixture of the various gradients of the social scale in the persons of its members, who number about fifty. Of three other clubs started last year, the Droylsden Alma has 22, the Fairfield Excelsior 16. and the Castle Victoria 14 members.

The mill holidays, in addition to Good Friday and Christmas Day, fluctuate considerably, yet generally consist of one or two days at New Year's tide, half a day on Easter Monday, about two days and a half at the close of Whit week, and the first three days at the wakes, besides break downs, &c.

Music must not be omitted. The Fairfield and Castle Brass Bands were organized and in active operation many years ago; but the former, like several successors, has ceased to practise. Several persons of late, especially Gaylard Hadwen, Esq., Joseph Hadwen, Esq., and Mr. Edward Chadwick, have been at pains to induce and encourage young folks to study the instrumental department of this delightful science, with the hope that its cultivation may render their homes more comfortable and happy. Two fife and drum bands have been connected with the Church Sunday School, but now lie dormant. A brass band in semi-connection with the same institution, under the auspices of Mr. Hadwen, was instituted July, 1857, and is now in a prosperous condition. Also within the district many an amateur violinist, &c., contrives to enliven leisure hours, which otherwise might hang heavy on his hands.

The vocal branch of the science has been studied, and its beauties and usefulness disseminated by the choirs of the several places of worship, by private amateurs, by various singing classes and societies in connection with the Church, Clayton Chapel of Ease, and the Independent Sunday Schools; and especially by Mr. C. H. Wrigley, late organist at the church, and the teacher and propagator in this district of the tonic sol-fa system of notation. The School Rooms or Chapels of Clayton, Edge-lane, and the New Connection possess harmoniums, which add to the solemnity of the services. Singing, music (organs, pianos, and violins), and dancing, form features of attraction at several of the public-houses. The Droylsden Philharmonic Society, established in November last for the purpose of encouraging the study of vocal and instrumental music, is under the fostering care of a committee, comprising the leading gentlemen of the village, and the conductorship of Mr. G. Eyles, of Fairfield, who intend creating an orchestra and chorus, capable of performing the best music and of undertaking concerts of a superior style. With this end in view, the spirited committee, in March last, purchased the Independent School Room for the purposes of meeting and practice.

THE RUSHBEARING.

The townships comprising the reputed chapelry of Newton—viz., Newton, Moston, Failsworth, and Droylsden—formerly, in a kind of quaternion, took their annual turn in the order above enumerated in providing the rushbearing to the chapel.

"The annual festivity of the four township chapelry" has been made the subject of a pleasing metrical sketch by Elijah Ridings, under the title of the "Village Festival." The rushbearing was held from time immemorial on the

Friday before the Sunday following the 18th of August. This vestige of the olden time has virtually sunk into desuetude; but as Droylsden's turn occurs this year most likely a rush cart will be built at some public-house, not however for the purpose of adding to the comfort of any place of worship.

Droylsden's rush cart was always fabricated at Greenside, and in 1793 John Wood, of Clayton Hall farm, provided rushes, waggon, and eight stumptailed horses to draw it from that hamlet to Newton. Few complete brass bands were then in existence; but, by gleaning in Gorton, Manchester, and other places, an extemporised company of instrumentalists was formed. Owing to dissensions in 1817, a rush cart was made at the White Hart, in opposition to the orthodox pageant at Greenside.

The last rush cart manufactured in Droylsden, in 1855, perambulated the village, and patronised Manchester, but did not visit Newton at all. In a waggon or cart was constructed a coned and symmetrical pyramid, faced with bolts of green rushes, and filled up with dried ones, and was decorated with ribbons, flowers, and a glittering display of silver plate. The procession was headed by the chapel garland, borne by men proud of their office; then came the music and morris dancers :—

> "All young fellows, blithe and hearty—
> Thirty couples in the party—
> Bedeck'd in gaudiest profusion,
> With ribbons in a sweet confusion,
> Of brilliant colours, richest dyes,
> Like wings of moths and butterflies,—
> Waving white kerchiefs in the air,
> And crossing here, recrossing there;
> And up and down, and everywhere."

The dancers were gorgeously decorated, as the young women emulated each other in procuring ribbons and other rustic finery for trimming the hats and shirts of their brothers or sweethearts. Then, amidst the cracking of whips and the huzzaing of the populace, came the rush cart, drawn by horses with "poseys," or garlands, affixed to their bridles; and then the instrumentalists—

> "Now, strike up music, the old tune;
> And louder, quicker, old bassoon;
> Come bustle, lads, for once dance more;
> And then cross morris three times o'er."

Arriving at the chapel, willing hands dismantled the cart, carried the rushes inside, and spread them beneath the forms on the earthen floor, as sings the poet—

> "The rushes on the chapel floor
> Are spread in time for winter's cold
> To warm the feet of young and old,
> When simple hearts the sacred lays
> Chaunt to our great Creator's praise."

The garland was placed in the interior of the chapel. Four beams projected between the windows on the north side, one of which appertained to each township for the purpose of displaying, for four years, the garland which had preceded its rushbearing. The garland consisted of a wooden framework, several yards in circumference, ornamented with artificial flowerets, cut in divers coloured papers, and surmounted either with a tinsel crown or the imitation of a bird, conventionally treated. Each township, as its turn came round, every fourth year, fetched out its old garland, and, by dint of reconstruction and improvement, attempted to surpass all previous efforts of the rival villages. On the following, or Wakes Sunday, the dancers, arrayed in their ribbons and finery, attended the Chapel, where an appropriate sermon was preached.

THREEDYWHEEL.

A singular wakes custom was introduced into Droylsden about 1814, from Woodhouses, where it had been prevalent for more than a third of a century. Chambers, in his "Edinburgh Journal," of November 19, 1824, gives it a notice, as does also Bell, under the title of the "Greenside Wakes Song," in his annotated edition of the "English Poets," recently published.

The ceremonial issued from Greenside, and consisted of two male equestrians grotesquely habited. One, John, son of Robert Hulme, of Greenside, personified a man; the other, James, son of Aaron Etchells, of Edge-lane, a woman.

They were engaged with spinning wheels, spinning flax in the olden style, and conducting a rustic dialogue in limping verse, and gathering contributions from spectators. Latterly a cart was substituted for a saddle, as being a safer position in case they grew tipsy. Both Bell and Chambers translate the rhyme into "gradely English," and render Threedywheel *tread the wheel ;* but it is evidently *thread the wheel*, as will be seen by a perusal of the original idiomatic and more spirited version :—

"It's Dreighlsdin wakes, un wey're commin to teawn,
To tell yo o' somethin' o' great reneawn ;
Un iv this owd jade ull lemmi begin,
Aw'l show yo heaw hard un heaw fast aw con spin.

Chorus.
So it's threedywheel, threedywheel, dan, don, dill, doe.

Theau brags o' thisel' ; bur aw dunno' think it true,
For aw will uphowd thi faurts arn't o few ;
For when theau hast done, un spun very hard,
O' this aw'm weel sure, thi work is ill marr'd.

Chorus.—So it's threedywheel, &c.

Theau saucy owd jade theaudst best howd thi tung,
Or else awst be thumpin' thi ere it be lung ;
Un iv ot aw do, theaurt sure for to rue,
For aw con ha' monny o one as good as you.

Chorus.—So it's threedywheel, &c.

What is it to me whoe you can have ?
Aw shanno be lung ere aw'm laid i' my grave ;
Un when aw am deod yo may foind, iv yo con,
One ot'll spin os hard os aw've done.

Chorus—So it's threedywheel, &c.

Com, com, mi dear woife, here eendeth mi sung.
Aw hope it has pleost this numerous thrung ;
Bur iv it has mist, yo needn't to fear,
Wey'll do eawr endeavour to pleos um next year.

Chorus.
So it's threedywheel, threedywheel, dan, don, dill, doe."

SUPERSTITION—FEEORIN' AND BOGGARTS.

Prior to the influx of inhabitants caused by the development of the cotton trade, the lives and actions of the rude and unlettered, but social and hospitable villagers, were considerably influenced by superstitious auguries drawn

from dreams and omens, as accidental variations from ordinary routine were considered, and from unshakable faith
in visions, spectres, and other supernatural agencies; whilst
few sombre or out-o'th'-way places, retired nooks and
corners, or sequestered bypaths, escaped the reputation of
being haunted. Many domiciles, also, had their presiding
boggart, and feeorin' swarmed at every turn of the dark old
lanes, and arch boggarts held revel at every three road end.

After dusk each rustle of the leaves, or sigh of the nightwind through the branches, to the timid wayfarer, heralded
the instant and unceremonious appearance of old wizards
and witches, Nut Nans and Clap Cans, or the terrific exploits of headless trunks, alias "men bout yeads," or other
traditionary "sperits," hobgoblins, and sprites, or the startling semblances of black dogs, phantoms, and other indescribable apparitions. Aqueous nymphs, or nixes, yclept
Grindylow and Jenny Greenteeth, lurked at the bottom of
pits, and with their long sinewy arms dragged in and
drowned children venturing too near. On autumnal evenings, the lambent flickering flame (carburetted hydrogen,
spontaneously ignited) of the "Corpse Candle," "Will o'
th' Wisp," or "Jack" or "Peg-a-Lantern" (for the sex was
not clearly ascertained), performed his or her fantastic and
impossible jumps, in the plashy meadows near Edge-lane,
to the terror of many a simple minded rustic. Fairies, also,
were believed to commit many depredations, such as eating
the children's porridge, nocturnally riding out the horses,
loosing the cows in the shippon, or churning the milk,
whilst "calving" by the fireside, and stealing the butter; and
hence behind many a door, as yet observable in Clayton,
both of dwelling and shippon, was carefully nailed a worn
horse shoe, believed to be a potent countercharm or talisman to their freaks and fancies.

There were certain localities in the township notorious as
the rendezvous or favourite promenades of boggarts and
feeorin', which, after nightfall had set in, few persons could
muster pluck sufficient to linger in, or even pass by, for

"Grey Superstition's whisper dread
Debarr'd the spot to vulgar tread."

Manifestly pre-eminent was "th' owd Green Lone," which
"Jem Hill, th' king o' Dreighlsdin," used to assert
"swaarmt wi fairees, witches, un boggarts, un which nob'dy
could mester bur hissel'." The boggart located at Thacker-
gate, near Alderdale, has well nigh scared many a sober
person out of his senses. Herds of four footed boggarts
used to issue from a pit at East End, and in form resembled
"great big dhogs, wi' great glearin' een os big os tay cups."
The patron boggart at the croft tenter's lodge, (South) Clockhouse, as fancy dictated, stalked through the chamber and
stripped the bed clothes off the sleepers, or, assuming gigantic
proportions and snow white vestments, perched in the solemn
yew, a strong and fearful contrast. At last, being exorcised
by an array of divines, it was *laid for a time*, beneath its
favourite tree. A field path from Fairfield to Ashton Hill-
lane was nightly traversed by a being of another world,
usually representing a shadowy lady, draped according
to whim, either in a loose white robe or otherwise in black
rustling silk. For a certain distance she glided in advance
of the pedestrian, and then by suddenly vanishing or disappearing from sight most likely left his hair standing on
end. At one of the Greenside farms, a murder was said to
have been committed in the shippon, and the exact spot was
supposed to be indicated by the impossibility of securely
fastening a cow in one particular boose; for, however carefully its occupant was chained overnight, next morning she
was sure to be found at large, and one time was actually
discovered on the shippon balks. Thither, it was believed
the cow had been carried by supernatural agency; but, be
that as it may, with the aid of blocks and ropes she was
cautiously lowered down. At a cottage adjoining, a boggart
varied its amusements by drumming on the old oaken chest,
still preserved, or, growing emboldened, shook the hangings
of the bed, or rustled amongst the clothes, the alarmed
occupants, sometimes, in despair, rolling up the coverlet,
and unavailingly whirling it at their invisible tormentor.
At a neighbouring farm house, amongst other vagaries, the
boggart would snatch up the infant, whilst asleep between
its parents, and, without awaking them, would harmlessly

deposit it on the hearthstone downstairs. In days gone by, few old halls and moated mansions were unconnected with the legendary lore

> " Of lovers' slights, and ladies' charms,
> Of witches' spells, of warriors' arms."

And of course " Clayton Ho " was honoured with a boggart, which, at dead of night, diversified its pranks by snatching the clothes from the beds, trailing heavy iron weights on the floors, or rattling endless chains through the crazy apartments. Becoming insufferable, the aid of a clergyman from the parish church was obtained; and, fortunately, with the aid of counterspells and incantations, he succeeded in laying the spirit for ever, declaring that—

> " Whilst ivy and holly are green,
> Clayton Hall boggart shall be no more seen."

Even yet, one room in the mansion is named the " bloody chamber," from some supposed stains of human gore on the oaken floor planks, but which, in reality, are only natural red tinges of the wood, denoting the presence of iron. According to the popular notions these tell tales silently commemorated some barbarous and forgotten act of remote times, and were irremoveable either by the art of the house-wife or carpenter. And, finally, even since the formation of the new road, J. W., the last of the ancient race of boggart seers in the township, used to combat with feeorin', between East End and Droylsden tollgate; but dying a few years ago, without making a legacy of the gift, he, happily, carried with him his mantle to the grave.

At a period just within memory, oft, after sunset, has the weary and tardy pedestrian quickened his speed on gaining proximity to some lonely place by suddenly remembering how, as suited a capricious taste, *the* tutelar " spirit" could appear as a rabbit or dog, a bear, or some outlandish and invincible animal which would fairly have puzzled the most skilful zoologist to have named or classified. When an inter-view, as was believed, did take place, the stoutest heart ever quaked, the strongest nerve ever quailed, and the boldest, whether man or woman, sought safety in flight, and, what with fear and exertion, often reached home entirely exhausted. Next day, to be sure, a flaming account of the adventure—a rich treat for the gossips, both male and female—was extensively circulated through the thinly populated locality, detailing at length, and gathering minuteness and improvement with transmission, how "Owd Yethurt o' Grunsho," or "Lung Tum woife th' neet ofore'r welly ta'en bi o great big black boggart, wi' great lung hurms, un whiskin' tail, yure as black as soote, un rowlin' een os big os sausurs."

On those winter evenings when the bow and the shuttle were at rest, whilst a youngster lolled on each hob, the sire, in his massive elbow chair, sat at the head of a semi-circle, by the blaze of a cheerful fire, formed jointly of billets of wood, peat turves, and coal. For a moment peep at the substantial, well made furniture, all of British oak, and black with the "elbow grease" of the mothers and grandmothers of generations gone by : the "one fingered" eight day clock ; the ancient chest, or wardrobe, preserving the bulk of the family clothing, with initials and date of the seventeenth century carved in relief by the artisan, half joiner, half carver, who made it ; the oaken couch chair ; the cupboard opening in the wall and displaying its rows of pewter plates and trenchers ; the bookshelf laden with tomes of old divinity, herbal, and chap books ; and on the walls prints and pictures commemorating events long past. And now the drowsy company ruminates over the gossip of the day ; then relates tales and legends of times past, and after the interspersal of a song or two, finally concludes with the supernatural. And now with open mouth and dilated eyes, with strained ears and excited brain, they draw nearer to the fire, whilst the aged parent retails many an ancient and oft told tradition of ghosts and haunted places, or narrates reminiscences of personal encounters with boggarts and feeorin'. At length, when the hour is grown late, almost scared out of their wits, they retire in a group upstairs, and ugly dreams debar their usual placid repose.

In those days, as is well known, the generality of persons were ignorant and unlettered ; and their corporeal employ-

ment not being counterbalanced by mental action, their
fallow imaginations consequently produced only crops of
superstition. The decadence of those old superstitions is to
be attributed to a variety of causes : straight, well paved
roads, increased intellectual activity in useful channels, railways frictionising the minds of one locality with the ideas
of another, the publication of scientific works, and, lastly,
as an aged recusant believer shrewdly remarked, a powerful agent in the explosion of those old notions was the
introduction of " Owd Ned un lung chimblies, fact'ry folk
havin' somat elze mind nur wandrin' ghosts un rollickin'
'sperits.'" And the same authority archly declared as a
clincher, "Ther' are no boggarts neaw, un iv ther' were,
folk un grown so wacken they'd catch um."

But it must not be imagined that superstition is lost ; its
form only has changed. For instance, the autumn of 1854
was remarkable, in Droylsden, for a prevalent mania for
mesmeric feats and delusions, which was engendered and
turned to good account by some artful charlatans. But
the deceptions practised became so alarming that a public
meeting was called, and, a warm discussion ensuing, the
village was shortly afterwards evacuated, and the event
was celebrated by "stangriding" the effigies of the chief
impostors.

AGRICULTURE.

The land of the township generally, excepting Clayton
Hall, is broken into small sized farm holdings, which,
consequently, are sub-divided into diminutive fields and
enclosures. The fields were once smaller than now, from
whence may be inferred that in times past there existed a
considerable agricultural population. Before the extension
of the cotton business the cottages were far outnumbered
by the farmsteads, and the inhabitants were engaged in an
admixture of trade and agriculture. The farming department, which only supplied milk and butter for the dairy,
was considered least remunerative, and, therefore, neglected
in favour of the buckhouse, the plank, and the loom. The
land is let at nearly its highest value, and even that portion

used exclusively for agricultural purposes commands several times the rental of a century ago.

One tendency to a pernicious agricultural result has arisen from the landowners anticipating that the progress of manufacturing enterprise might shortly render their farms the nucleus of building speculations, and thereby productive of high chief rents. They have preferred letting them on the year to year system in lieu of the lease principle, which alone can stimulate a tenant to thorough cultivation. Again, a long prevalent, though mistaken, notion recognises the necessity of a seven years' apprenticeship to almost every calling except that of a farmer. Everybody has been supposed to know, by some intuitive instinct, how to purchase and attend to live stock, manage the multifarious systems of drainage and irrigation, pursue the best rotation of crops and culture of artificial grasses, with the right changes of seed and applications of manure. Hence, amongst other anomalies to deplore, hollow draining, whether by tiles or sod, has only partially succeeded guttering by the spade or water furrowing with the plough. Bone, guano, and other artificial manures are almost unknown, and fields exhausted by grain crops have been laid down to grass with "nothing in their belly," whence arises the continuance of land in a state of comparative infertility.

The soil is chiefly a strong, heavy loam, on a substratum of stiff, ferruginous clay, and much of it comparatively sterile, with little energy expended on its cultivation. Corn growing and tillage husbandry, as a necessary result of the influx of population, have been superseded by meadows and grazing land for the dairy. It appears that sheep never abounded in the township, the soil having been too damp and marshy and the climate too humid to suit their constitutions. And amongst black cattle, in Droylsden, as elsewhere, for more than a century past, fatal diseases have been periodically epidemic. Hence, a Cow Club was established in 1805, at the Fairfield New Inn, from whence, in 1848, it was removed to the Openshaw New Inn. Formerly, cheese making, for home consumption, slightly prevailed, and butter making was common ; and at present Mr. Grange, of Greenside, calves and churns the entire milk of his dairy of twenty-five cows, by means of a steam engine of four horse power! With almost this exception, milk production monopolises the farmers' attention, who retail it at 2½d. per quart, and supply small quantities of fresh butter, churned from overplus milk, at 1s. 2d. per pound the year through.

Although grass, or hay, is the chief product of the fields, yet plough cultivation raises, to a slight extent, wheat, oats, potatoes, and turnips, as also mangel wurtzel, vetches, clover, and other requisites for farm consumption. Summer fallowing was superseded by potato planting, and for more than four score years cotters have planted these tubers by spade husbandry, providing the seed and manure, and paying at the rate of from 9d. to 1s. per rod of forty-nine square yards, for the use of the land, the cartage of the manure to and the crop from the field. The entire surface of the township now under tillage is computed at not more than twenty customary Lancashire acres.

Formerly, lime was very expensive, having to be fetched by pack horses from a distance, and, consequently, marl, which contains carbonate of lime, as a cheap substitute, had for ages been applied as manure for tillage lands, preparatory to wheat sowing, and proved useful when peaty soils were much more abundant than now. Most of the old pitsteads yet extant in the fields have been quarries whence this mineral has been obtained. Within recollection of the oldest inhabitants several marl pits have been formed in the township, and from them the following particulars are gleaned:—The "gaffer" of the pit, who controlled the falls and excavations, was honoured, *pro tem.*, with the distinguishing appellation of "My Lord." Passers by and casual spectators were solicited to contribute to the "marl shutting," or feast at the conclusion of their labours, and, if an individual only gave a sixpence it was vauntingly proclaimed, accompanied by beating the drum, purposely kept in the pit, that "Mr. George Green, Esquire, had given a largess of silver," or otherwise it was acknowledged as "a part of a thousand pounds." Notwithstanding skill and precaution, fatal accidents were not uncommon. Joseph

Beswick, of Droylsden, who was killed in Mr. Edmundson's
marl pit, was buried at Ashton in July, 1684, and Ann
Taylor, who also was killed in a marl pit, in August, 1767,
is noticed incidentally in the poor rate books. Marl was
generally applied to land at the back end of the year, at the
rate of from five to eight cubic rods per acre, and was spread
by the unloader, commonly designated "Old Crow," or
" Lord Crow," who cast it in spadefuls from the cart. After
proper subjection to the "falling" processes of the united
agency of frost and rain, the mineral was ploughed into the
earth. When the last spring corn had been sown, the
festival called "marl shutting," or "marl guising," was
annually celebrated. In addition to a profusion of meat
and drink, singing and dancing, and other concomitants of
merry making, there was a custom of " rustling," or shaking
in the hat for ribbons, which the fortunate winners arranged
round their hats, and wore on their heads, whilst resorting
to church on the Sunday following.

Notwithstanding the trouble and expense consequent on
marl getting, little attention seems to have been paid to the
collection and proper distribution of farmyard manure, as
the middens were allowed to stand undisturbed, except
by fresh accumulations, for years, until they were grassed
over in the folds, and appeared like meadows.

Amongst cereal products rye and barley were once slightly
raised, but the soil was too heavy and cold for their successful cultivation. Oats were the principal crop, and hence
were emphatically designated " corn," and, though now
superseded in usefulness by wheat, they still retain this
distinction. Oat cakes were once the staple article of diet,
and were stored on wooden fleaks suspended from the
ceiling, without which implements the furniture of cottages,
and even farm houses, was considered incomplete. Jannock,
a loaf made of coarse oatmeal and leavened, was held also in
general estimation. Oats were given to the horses, which,
though possessed by few of the small farmers, yet at
Clayton no less than twelve teams were kept all the year
round for the duties of the farm.

Although not a single sheaf of wheat is now grown in the

hamlet of Clayton, yet there, as in the rest of the township, it was once extensively raised. When John Wood removed from the Hall, in 1793, there were 100 acres sown with this cereal, of which, in the autumn following, he claimed one half the crop from the summer worked land. Amongst the good ploughmen of those days were Lawrence Cash and Elias Bethel, men who, contrary to modern custom, had regularly " served their time to farming " at Clayton Hall.

Rejoicings when all the grain had been housed, elsewhere called " Harvest Homes," were unknown to this locality ; but similar frolics, termed " kurn shuttin's"—*i.e.*, corn quittings—followed the conclusion of reaping, or wheat shearing. The "kurn shuttin' " earliest in season now recollected, was celebrated at Clayton Hall, on the 30th July, 1826, which was, also, the hottest summer remembered. Two other designations for the feast were "churn getting" and "churn supper," so named from the introduction of a churn containing a good supply of cream, which was circulated by dishfuls to each of the company, who ate it with bread. After the custom of cream eating fell into desuetude, the churn, with a sickle in it, still continued to be produced at table. The leader of the reapers, who usually attained his position through merit, was addressed by his associates as " My Lord," and became an important personage at the feast, being held responsible for the decorum of the guests. A most momentous preliminary consisted in his heading a procession of the band of reapers to that side of the fold, or homestead, on which lay a farm where the corn was either wholly or partially uncut, when, to attract attention, they first swung round their hats, and shouted at the top of their voices, " Whoo ! whoo ! whoop ! " Then the leader, or his deputy, mounted on a tub, and exclaimed—

> " O yes ! O yes ! O yes ! *
> Daniel Ogden's getten sick a churn ;
> We'll turn out th' hare i' Joe Green's kurn."

Lastly, followed a right hearty shout, after which, augmented by the family, friends, and domestics, of the farmer,

---

* A corruption of *oyez*, Norman French, meaning, *hear ye.*

they adjourned to partake of a substantial supper and un-
stinted supply of ale. If any man flagged in the "drinking
bout" that followed, which, at the farmer's expense, often
lasted through the night, the rest gathered round him,
exclaiming as well as able —

> " Drink, boys, drink !
>   Mind and don't spill ;
>   For if you do,
>   You must drink two,
>   For that's your master's will."

If he still remained obdurate, the contents of the cup, or
jug, were generally poured down his jacket sleeves.

NATURAL PRODUCTIONS.

The site of Droylsden has been in past ages entirely a
woodland tract, for even the Moss constitutes but the grave
of a forest. Within memory, the dwellings nestled amongst
sheltering trees, the hedgerows were well shaded with
timber, and the several lane roads were arched over with
noble oaks, the growth of long centuries. Dingle Wood, in
Clayton, and the various cloughs and dells, brooksides and
slopes descending to the Medlock, abounded with under-
wood, among which were interspersed tufts of majestic
oaks, a few stately ash, and trees of other varieties. Many
of the oaks ranged from six to twelve feet in circumference ;
and one of the finest furnished both water wheel and the
other implements for the Corn Mill at Clayton.

The present local scarcity of timber has arisen from the
necessities of the landlords, from its increased value, and
from once having been regarded as fuel, as well as used for
the purposes of building and carpentry. The indigenous
trees now extant are principally sproutlings from ancient
stocks, and, as well as those naturalised, are limited in kind,
and incompetent in size almost to perform the functions of
a gate stump.   Chief are oaks, then ash, willow, alder,
sycamore, elm, birch, mountain ash, and some poplars,
unsightly in appearance, and almost valueless as timber.
Small but thriving plantations embower Alderdale Lodge
and Clayton Hall.   Predominating amongst considerable

plantations on the Clayton estate are various kinds of firs, which, being unadapted to soil or climate, add little by their stunted growth to the perspective beauty of the locality.

Within memory hazel trees abounded on the Clayton estate ; and, as in fruitful seasons a burn of nuts could be gathered in " no time," a watch was set to deter parties, who came from Manchester early in the morning, and took sackfuls away at a time.

Crab trees were protected and encouraged, if not actually cultivated. Their yield was sometimes enormous, and the produce was taken to the Crushing Mill, in Audenshaw, and converted into verjuice, which was accounted a sovereign specific for procuring an appetite, and used in all families, both gentle and simple.

Formerly, attached to every dwelling, was an orchard well stocked with fruit trees ; and two orchards are expressly stated in the time of James I. as being appurtenant to the Edge-lane estate. Indeed, within memory, in addition to apple and pear trees, several varieties of plum—such as sugar, winter, greengage, and damson—were abundant in the orchards, and frequently lined the hedgerows bordering the farmsteads.

It is to be regretted that cottage gardening has not been carried out with the spirit it deserves. This, perhaps, arises from the clayey nature of the soil, which unfits it also for market gardens ; consequently, culinary vegetables are few in variety and poor in quality. Greenhouse plants are frequent in cottages, and nine out of a row of ten cottages at East End recently exhibited potted plants on their window sills.

Competitive floral and horticultural exhibitions, and prize shows, are annually devised at public-houses, and one has recently been established to meet in the Educational Institution ; but hitherto their tendency has been rather to encourage the purchase and procurement of specimens than the growth and local cultivation of the fruits and flowers, or plants and vegetables, themselves.

BOTANY.

The flora of the vicinity once boasted a considerable variety of indigenous herbs and plants, some of which were comparatively uncommon, but few of them rare. Several causes have led to their extirpation—the felling of trees and stubbing of the brushwood, the eradications of the spade and the plough, the cultivation of the Moss, and, lastly, the incursions of the Manchester herb doctors and botanists; for even the latter, in many cases, on discovering a choice plant have borne it away, both branch and root, in the proudest triumph.

Specimens of the following herbs and plants have been met with in the localties indicated, but most of them are now extinct. On the Moss were long leaved and round leaved sundews, marsh rosemary, marsh andromeda, yellow or Lancashire bog asphodel, small fumitory, water plaintain, wild carrot, common and cross leaved heaths, and the two varieties of cotton grass, the many headed and the single headed, or "moss crop." On Graver-lane farm were St. John's, or the flowering fern, lady and sweet scented ferns, brackens, &c. Wood sage and wood betony were exuberant on Bow Brow; corn campion, near the Strawberry Gardens; adders' tongue and devil's bit, at Waterside; figwort and wild raspberry, in Jericho Clough; blue hyacinth, soapwort, bistort, and perennial goosefoot, in Clayton Vale; arum, in Clayton Wood; bullrush, and yellow flag iris, in a pit near Edge-lane; water avens, in another near Buxton-lane; nipplewort, hartstongue, brooklime and Good King Henry (salads), and patience dock (an edible), near Waterhouses; and in the same vicinity flourish burdocks—the local "umbrellas" of children—and gipsy wort, used by those wanderers to stain the complexions of their children, as the old ditty inviteth—

> " Come stain your cheek with nut and berry,
> For the gipsies' life is merry."

A botanical society, as a sort of revival of one existing in Gorton a few years previously, was begun about 1825, in a chamber over a six loomed workshop, at Little Droylsden. This association, numbering about a dozen members, believing itself the nucleus of an important institution, assumed the high sounding title of the Lancashire Linnæan Society; and, in addition to botany, intended their studies and researches to embrace mineralogy, entomology, conchology, ornithology, &c. Meetings were held monthly, and on the Sunday. Each member in rotation was bound by the rules, which existed in MS., to describe a plant, either verbally or in writing, at every meeting. For a time prosperity awaited them, and friendly visits were paid by Joshua Hobson and other well known botanists. But after two or three years had elapsed, the members gradually neglected both subcription and attendance, and at last the society faded away.

NATURAL HISTORY, ETC.

Droylsden Mechanics' Institution was originated in 1842 as a Naturalists' Society. Mr. J. W. Slater, one of the founders, was an excellent naturalist, and delivered instructive lectures on that science and also upon botany, geology, entomology, &c. George Hill, a mill warper at Droylsden Mills, and brother of the Rev. William Hill, once sub-editor of the *Northern Star*, was curator to the institution for awhile. A limited exhibition of specimens in natural history, entomology, fossils, antiquities, &c., was held in 1843, and another in the spring of 1849; and both proved very successful.

The hand loom weavers of Little Moss and Woodhouses, hamlets adjoining to Droylsden, make entomology their leisure study and favourite recreative pursuit, sallying out at eventide for the procurement of moths, butterflies, and beetles. Principally from these sources, an exhibition chiefly of subjects in natural history, was organised by John Birtenshaw, of Square Fold, Droylsden, and held at the Railway Tavern (Mr. Howarth's) in the same township, remaining open from April to August, 1856. The exhibition contained, beside Russian trophies, ostrich eggs, &c., some beautiful and unique devices, worked in moths, butterflies, and beetles, the designs including peacocks, lizards,

&c. One of the chief attractions had for a centrepiece a balloon, wrought in a mosaic of butterflies and moths, and on each side was presented the representation of a tree, artistically formed of the various varieties of beetles.

The Byrons, like other families of gentle blood, were partial to the pleasures of the chase, and so early as June, 1308, Sir Richard de Byron is found obtaining a grant of "free warren" in Clayton demesne. The term "warren" included liberty to hunt and preserve game, and also the place in which, by the grant, they were privileged to keep beasts and fowls of warren. The Sir John Byron, whose name is associated with the legend of Little Droylsden, is traditionally reputed to have maintained two packs of hunting dogs. In the conveyance of the Clayton estate, in 1620, the "impaled ground called Clayton Park" is distinctly enumerated. Almost within recollection, the Manchester Old Hounds, a full mouthed (*i.e.*, noisy) variety, of which an engraving is inserted in Whitaker's "History of Manchester," hunted the locality embracing Droylsden. The Ashton Hunt, superintended by Squire Astley, had once famous hunting days in the township. About thirty years ago a pack of hounds was kept in Droylsden, the dogs being allotted for maintenance to the several lovers of the sport. Mr. Samuel Brundret kept a pack of beagles and a number of greyhounds for hunting and coursing purposes.

Both Clayton demesne and Waterside were once strictly preserved. Two enclosures in Clayton are yet named Coney Green and Coney Meadow; and, within memory, hares and rabbits, as well as pheasants and partridges, were anything but scarce in Clayton. In Dingle Wood a few herons have been met with; flocks of plovers and stock-doves were visitors; and lapwings, magpies, corncrakes, woodcocks, and crows, built their nests there. Bitterns, the local "bitterbump," and once an esteemed delicacy, which frequented only marshy places, gradually disappeared with the enclosure of the moss, the last being killed at Bow Brow, about seven years since. In addition to many of the foregoing birds, the moss was resorted to by land dottrels, water hens, coots, large and jack snipes, grey and golden plovers, wheatears, larks, wagtails, &c. The banks of the Medlock and Sunny Bank brook, were frequented by kingfishers and bullfinches, sand snipes, sand martins, long-wings, or swifts, and other varieties now extinct in the locality. Barn owls were plentiful; two varieties breeding at Clayton Hall, and patronising the farm houses at Sunny Bank, Yew Tree, and other places.

Blind worms were common; vipers are alleged to have lurked on the moss; and scores of adders were generally found on the removal of middens, which were often allowed to accumulate in the folds for years together.

Both flat fish and eels were abundant. The waters of the Medlock, then guiltless of refuse, dyes, and chemicals, were clear as gin, and "snied" with eels, trout, and chub. Many of the field pits, in addition to eels, contained English carp, bream, perch, and dace, whilst pike were preserved in Clayton Hall moat.

CROFTING, OR BLEACHING.

About the sixteenth century, trading enterprise began to share with pastoral occupations the time of the inhabitants; and bleaching thenceforward formed one of the staple employments of the village.

As, under the primitive system, crofting could only be effected in the summer months, during a third of the year outdoor operations had to be suspended. The general custom was to employ the men during winter in the yarnhouse, making-up; and in sending home what had been done in the summer, and fetching more for the ensuing season. The unmarried workmen usually lived altogether at the place of employment. The foreman received half a guinea a week and his maintenance. Work was customarily begun in summer at four a.m.; in winter, at daybreak; and ceased at six in the evening, supper being ready at seven, except on Saturday afternoon, when they left off at four o'clock.

The lin, or linen yarn, required nearly twelve months to bring it to a marketable state, until, in 1788, Mr. Thomas

E

Henry introduced the art of bleaching with oxymuriatic gas, or chlorine, which reduced the time requisite for completing the entire process to one or two days at most.

The first Manchester Directory (Elizabeth Raffald's), in 1773, contains an alphabetical list of the "whitsters," or bleachers, of the district, who numbered seventy-nine. A few years later, chiefly through the improved mode of treatment, and the consequent facilities for concentration, despatch, and extension of business, linen bleaching rapidly declined, the Directory of 1788, as compared with that of 1781, showing a decrease of no less than thirty-eight local bleacheries.

A renewal of the duty on salt took place in 1732, and the act remained unrepealed for ninety-one years. At a time when salt, for domestic purposes, was retailed at 4d. per pound, that commodity was allowed free of duty for manufacturing purposes; and, consequently, bleachers' carts were despatched to Northwich, where chemical agents were admixed with the salt, in order to render it unfit for household use.

Under the old system, for the greater portion of the year, many of the fields were whitened over with linen yarn in the process of bleaching. It was a common practice for the crofters not only to lay the materials on their own land, but also on that of their neighbours, the privilege being accorded in consideration of the fertilising properties of the soap, ashes, and other ingredients with which the yarn had been imbued. This exposure of so valuable a material proved a strong temptation to the cupidity of many; and hence, although watchmen were employed, croft breaking became quite a common occurrence. At length the Legislature interfered, and in 1731 passed an act specially "to prevent the stealing of linen, fustian, and other wares from the fields, where they are whitening, or drying." In 1786, James Holland was hanged on Bolton Moor, for croft breaking; and on the 15th of September, 1798, George Russell for a similar offence suffered a similar fate on Newton Heath, and was afterwards buried at Blackley Church. Several hundred pounds worth of yarn were stolen from Peter Shawcross, of Droylsden, who was instrumental in transporting two persons for the same offence.

Great consternation was excited amongst the dyers and bleachers in 1784, by the imposition of the "Fustian Tax," or duty of one penny per yard "upon all bleached cotton manufactures." But, owing to the pressure of public opinion, this impolitic act was repealed in the year following.

The names of John Redford, Edward Thornely, and John Grundy, occur about 1742, in Gorton Church-registers, as being whitsters resident in Droylsden; but there is nothing to determine whether they were masters or journeymen.

There appear to have been at least fifteen crofting concerns, or bleaching establishments, in active operation in the township; and, although in the course of gradual obliteration, yet, in some shape or other, many of the bowk or buck-houses, yarnhouses, ponds, holds, or reservoirs, are still remaining.

The farm at Greenside, which John Gibson now holds, was occupied for seventeen years by John Howarth, and, after his death in 1792, by his son Benjamin, both of whom were engaged in the bleaching business.

The farm a little lower down, and on the opposite side of the lane, now tenanted by Job Prestwich, was used as a crofting place, just a century ago, by Richard Hulme, and was continued, after his death, from 1784 to 1805 by his son Robert Hulme.

Passing down Greenside-lane, the farmstead cresting the knoll on the left is believed to have been a bleaching place. A century ago, Jacob Booth was the tenant, and in 1786 he was followed by Adam Bowker; but neither of them are remembered to have been engaged in bleaching.

The next farm over the way was used for crofting. William Blackshaw, son of Thomas Blackshaw, a bleacher in Edge-lane, crofted here for fifteen years prior to 1784, when he was followed by William Howarth, of Prestwich, who purchased the estate. He was the last bleacher here, and operated on both linen and cotton yarns. Being a careful thrifty man, he built some cottages, dubbed "Leawsy Bonk," in Greenside-lane, and left by will several thousand pounds.

Once more recrossing the lane, the (North) Clockhouse is

thought to have been a bleachery. However, in 1786, the occupant, Philip Berry, was attending to agriculture alone.

Bridge End farm was occupied by James Heape prior to 1761, when John Pott became tenant. Dying in 1795, and leaving his eldest son *non compos mentis*, the charge of the crofting concern devolved on his son George, who, at death, bequeathed a pound per week to his elder brother. During George's occupancy, the canal burst its banks near the copperas works, and the water, rushing along the brook, washed down the bowkhouse at Bridge End, after which he declined bleaching in favour of manufacturing. Joshua Barratt, who followed Pott, about 1808, resumed the bleaching of linen yarn, and began, as he had previously done at Abbey Hey, Gorton, to size cotton in the bundle. He was the last crofter here, and discontinued business about forty years since.

On the site of the mansion at Alderdale stood a farm house of a superior description to any in the locality, which was occupied, in 1745, by Abraham Beswick, who was followed by his son, Samuel Beswick, who resided here in 1776 and up to 1806. At one end of the building were kennels for a number of dogs, kept for shooting purposes; and above, ascended by an external flight of steps, was the bed chamber for the workmen. Unlike any other work in the township, the principal portion of the bleaching done here consisted of candlewicking, made of the refuse in cloth making from Hambro' yarn, so called from the name of the place whence imported. This waste was cleansed from dirt by thrashing it with a flail, then watered, trodden with the feet, and beaten on large flags with mallets of wood, and afterwards passed through the usual processes.

On the same side of Edge-lane, and where William Parkinson now farms, in 1746 lived Thomas Blackshaw, who carried on crofting till his failure, thirty years afterwards. Peter Shawcross succeeded him, and continued here till his death, in December, 1811, following, as usual, both farming and crofting. In addition to bleaching linen, Mr. Shawcross had the honour of introducing cotton bleaching into the township.

A short occupation road, on the same side of the lane, leads to the farm now held by John Wolfenden ; and here, from 1759 to 1766, resided Widow Blackshaw ; and thence to 1771, John Blackshaw, probably her son, who followed the occupation of whitster. Then succeeded Sampson Ferrand, who, after struggling four or five years, failed in the business, which was never carried on again at this farm. Samuel Beswick then took the place, and carted yarns from Alderdale, to spread on the fields. After Beswick gave it up, Thomas Barlow, his son-in-law, farmed it till his death, in August, 1826. During a part of the time (say sixty years ago), Barlow was successfully engaged in dyeing fancy hats, or rather females' bonnets, in Devonshire browns and sky blue.

Sunny Bank was employed as a crofting place by John Blackshaw, in 1741, and up to his death, about eighteen years afterwards, when Margaret, his widow, continued the farming, but relinquished the bleaching department.

The small estate, on part of which Edge-lane Mill is erected, appears to have been used for bleaching operations prior to 1617, when one of the fields was known as the Yarncroft.

Yew Tree farm is said to have been used as a crofting place by the family of Grimshaw. The registers at Gorton notice James Grimshaw, whitster, in 1711; Thomas, in 1743-6; and Joshua, in 1748, all of Droylsden; but there is nothing to indicate whether they were masters or workmen, or whether resident at Yew Tree or not.

The (South) Clockhouse farm, as far back as the reign of James I., was employed in bleaching operations by the family of Hall, the last of whom, John Hall, continued resident till about 1760, when Jervis Travis seems to have succeeded him, and continued here for at least thirteen years. In 1775 John Travis was apparently tenant, and resided here up to about 1805 or 1806, when he left the village. Travis did an extensive business, chiefly in bleaching linen yarns, and was the last person who followed that occupation at this farm.

Birch Fold was once a bleachery, the bowkhouse having

only been removed a few years ago. However, in 1785, the tenant, John Schofield, applied himself solely to farming.

Round Oak farm, now Fairfield estate, was held in 1745, by Thomas Bertenshaw, crofter, who was the last person here so employed. The bowkhouse was converted into a cottage, and as such is still in existence.

THE HAT MANUFACTURE.

Under the term "feltmaker" occurs the first allusion to hat manufacture in the township, when, in 1700, John Hall, of Droylsden, feltmaker, was buried at Gorton Chapel. About the close of last century, a description of hat was made here from white Spanish wool, coney wool, and camel's hair, and covered with beaver; the price for body making, up to the dyeing process, running from thirty shillings to thirty-two shillings per dozen. At that time a well finished stuff hat was worth from a guinea to twenty-three shillings, and nearly "lasted a man's life."

Although a considerable number of operatives or journeymen have resided in Droylsden, yet few employers have located themselves. James Turner, in 1814-25, farmed a portion of the present Fairfield Mills estate, and also manufactured hats to a slight extent. Mr. John Wood commenced the business in Fairfield, and a few years afterwards, in 1820, took into co-partnership Mr. Charles Cordingley. At the end of eleven years a dissolution took place, when Mr. Wood commenced the business, unsuccessfully, in Openshaw, and Mr. Cordingley erected the premises he still occupies as a hat warehouse at Spring Bank. About 1828, this firm manufactured one hundred dozens of plated hats weekly. Mr. Simon Harker, previously of Audenshaw, in 1823-5, carried on the business at Green-lane, in Droylsden.

SKETCH OF THE EARLY COTTON TRADE.

Formerly the only trades struggling in the district were linen hand loom weaving, crofting, or bleaching, and feltmaking, or hatting.

From time immemorial linen weaving had been pursued as an auxiliary employment to agriculture, and almost

every farmstead had its loom house attached. In the
middle of the seventeenth century, Humphrey Chetham, of
Clayton Hall, and in the reign of George I., George
Grimshaw, of Edge-lane, followed the business of chapmen
—*i.e.*, merchants in a small way, or general dealers in
cotton linen fustians, made from linen warps and cotton
weft.

The first record of textile manufactures in connection
with Droylsden is in 1697, when John Woosencroft, of
Edge-lane, earned a livelihood as "linen webster," in
addition to holding a small farm. The overseers used to
apprentice many parish lads to linen weavers; and in the
corresponding year of last century, they paid premiums
amounting in the aggregate to nearly eleven pounds with
four youths so bound. As showing the proportion of workpeople of various trades, a list of poor and infirm for nearly
thirty years later, 1778, may be quoted. It includes seventeen weavers, nine hatters, two crofters, a bleacher, a
carrier, a shoemaker, and a blacksmith.

Reliable information respecting the cotton trade in
Droylsden extends back only to the year 1776, at which
period the handicraft, or manufacture, was in its domestic
stage, and confined to the fireside and cottage. The spinning procedure was as follows :—First, the raw cotton was
washed through a lather of sweet soap, wrung out with a
screw press, and dried in a stove, or on a fleak exposed to
the sun or fire. Next, the cotton underwent an operation
technically termed "batting and picking." A woman, with
smooth flexible rods or switches in each hand, beat the
cotton on a square wooden frame, across which were tightly
stretched a number of small cords, with openings sufficient
to permit the expelled seed, leaves, and other adventitious
matter to drop through. In the process succeeding, by
holding a hand card firmly on her knee, with batted cotton
placed thereon, and, taking another card into her right
hand, she dexterously carded it into soft loose rolls of about
the thickness of a candle, and from eight to twelve inches
long. Next followed the "slubbing," which was performed
by means of the one spindle wheel. The operator twisted

one end of a carding round the point of the spindle, to
which revolutionary movement was imparted by the slub-
ber's right hand, through turning the band wheel, whose
rim was some five feet in diameter, whilst, at the same time,
holding the other end between the finger and thumb of the
left hand, she rapidly drew out the slubbing horizontally by
pacing back to the extent of her reach. After stopping
until the necessary spiral twist had been given to the
coarse, round, and soft thread (called a "slubbing," but
similar to that now denominated a "roving"), she wound
it on the spindle, and continued the process until the cop
was large enough to be taken off. Generally, this operation
of drawing and twisting was repeated, whereby the slubbing
was converted into a smaller, finer, and longer thread; and
to this latter operation the term "spinning" was more
properly applied.

About four score years ago, James Stanley, a Droylsdenian, married a woman from Glossop, who, as part of her
dowry, brought him a spinning jenny* of twenty spindles.
It remained inactive till her death, a year or two afterwards,
when it was brought into requisition by the wife of one
Abraham Taylor, who consequently became the first jenny
spinner in the township. Previously, on the one spindle
system, one good weaver could keep three active women
spinners at work; but the case was reversed by the above
improved machine, which easily afforded a supply for three
weavers. Upon this frame, at the rate previously paid,
the spinner could comfortably have earned half a guinea per
day. For some time after the introduction of the jenny,
the old mode of slubbing, or roving, on the single spindle
continued in use. The joining of the rolls, or cardings,
though made longer than formerly, rendered manual dex-
terity absolutely necessary. Subsequently, many novel and
ingenious contrivances for accelerating labour were in-
vented; but want of space forbids almost their bare enumeration. A gradual extension in the size of spinning and

---

* Gin—a very early word for an engine, or machine;
it occurs in that sense in Psalm cxl. 5.

preparatory machinery, as well as its concentration, and that of the workpeople, rendered dwelling houses inconvenient, and larger premises for spinning became requisite, whilst weaving, as heretofore, was continued in small rooms or apartments. About the year 1780, there were in the township a number of families who, within their own limits, prepared, carded, spun, warped, and wove fustians, and goods of a similar type, each cottage thus forming an independent miniature factory. The privileges of the spinning jenny being wholly given up to the public in the year 1785, a few energetic and spirited persons in the township turned their attention to spinning cotton on what was then considered an extensive scale, and exhibited far more enterprise in the business than had previously been displayed in the cultivation of the soil.

Robert Booth, in May, 1785, reared his premises adjoining the White Hart, which, besides being the first three storeyed building, was also, properly speaking, the first primitive factory in the township, possessing, as it did, spacious rooms entirely devoted to the business. Entering into partnership with one Swindells, Booth commenced spinning; but after carrying on a short time, the partnership was dissolved and the trade was relinquished, although Booth survived until August, 1798, when he died in his sixtieth year.

About 1786, or soon after, Mr. Joseph Mallalieu occupied one end, and Mr. Radley the other, of the attic in a three storeyed building in Fairfield, now the residence of Mr. Anslow. This establishment, so far as moving power went, was a joint concern, the machinery in both portions being turned by a large wheel, or gin, placed in a low building adjacent, and turned round by one *bonâ fide* HORSE power, driven by a lad. In Mr. Mallalieu's concern, after the necessary preparations, the cotton was passed through fluted cards, and then transferred to the roving frame, or "cotton billy," which was driven by hand, and through which the cardings were drawn by means of a series of rollers and an endless inclined plane composed of linen cloth. The work of the piecer to the "billy" was very arduous; he had to

E 3

watch each carding attentively; and twist another to the end of it; and woe betide him if he permitted a carding to slip through the rollers, for the rovers used their piecers with great severity. These latter were children of seven, or even six, years of age, and were employed from six a.m., or earlier, to eight or nine p.m., or later, at wages varying from 1s. 6d. to 2s. 6d. per week. The rovings were passed through the "slubbing jenny," and then spun by hand (piecers under ten years of age receiving 4s. per week), and afterwards converted into warps, which were sold for manufacturing into fustians. Mr. Radley used his portion of the factory for spinning only, and the operatives he employed were young women, natives of various parts of Yorkshire.

Mr. Henry Nalty afterwards erected the building now used as the young gentlemen's boarding school, for the purpose of spinning in, the rovings being obtained from Mr. Joseph Mallalieu's concern. The mule here in use contained no less than twelve dozen spindles; and the novelty of so large a number of spindles being turned by hand brought many curious persons to inspect it.

Mr. Frank Mallalieu, father to Mr. F. C. Mallalieu, of Fairfield, in partnership with Mr. Henry Nalty, begun a spinning establishment, about 1790, in the building since used for a time as the Boys' Sunday School; and subsequently, when Mr. Joseph Mallalieu discontinued the business, the concerns were united.

Sometime about the former period, the Sisters' House was enlarged for the purpose of receiving four mules of one hundred and forty-four spindles each.

There was yet another small establishment in Fairfield. The chamber of a dwelling house contained a "doubling jenny"; and in the room beneath a large hand mule was worked by an old man, who afterwards, being ill used by Mr. Cresswell, discontinued the employment.

Returning to Droylsden village, four concerns are found in operation about the year 1790. The largest was that of Mr. John Hammond, father of Mr. Hammond, of the New Inn, Openshaw, who built and resided at the three storeyed premises, now the Bull's Head, in King-street.

The carding machine, turned by a horse and gin, was located in the cottage adjoining, whilst the spinning was carried on in the garret of the house. At first Mr. Hammond employed spinning jennies ; but afterwards, about 1793-4, purchased the first machine termed "a mule" on this side of Manchester.

John Blackshaw lived at the house up three steps opposite the new Independent Chapel, and spun upon jennies on the second floor.

Joseph Lowe and his brother erected a dwelling house, now replaced by the shop held by Mrs. Parker, pawnbroker, and commenced supplying twist and weft to Mr. Cresswell, of Fairfield. The brother dying, Joseph Lowe, who had married a daughter of Robert Booth, deserted his own place in favour of his father-in-law's premises, near the White Hart. Like Blackshaw, Lowe had his carding and slubbing done by Ralph Wood, of Audenshaw.

William Hadfield spun upon jennies in his dwelling house, which adjoins the building lately used as the Temperance Room. Like the Lowes, he was chiefly engaged in spinning for Mr. Cresswell.

It is very remarkable that the whole of these concerns were discontinued within a few years. Various reasons are assigned. One was the bad trade and the requirement of men for soldiers, consequent on the breaking out of the French war : another, that some of the speculators were not noted for economy and frugality. Improvements came so fast upon them that they could not keep pace in purchasing new machines, and were consequently left in the rear of competition ; and so were compelled either to relinquish business or to fail. Be this as it may, some of them became bankrupt and the rest voluntarily resigned, leaving it for a few enterprising capitalists and practical men of business, foreigners to the soil, in more favourable times, to amass large fortunes by redeeming and perpetuating the manufacturing industrialism of the place.

COTTON WEAVING AND MANUFACTURING.

There were in Droylsden numerous weavers of cotton, linen, fustians, and checks, prior to 1780, soon after which an extraordinary impulse was imparted to cotton hand loom weaving, though only common checks, crossovers, calicoes, and a coarse and inferior kind of fabric were made. After much investigation, the following list of firms, and putters out in the township has been carefully compiled.

Mr. William Cresswell, fustian manufacturer, on the erection of Fairfield, removed his warehouse from Lees, near Oldham. After doing a very extensive business, owing partly to family improvidence, he failed in business about the year 1812, and removed to Devonport, where he died some dozen years ago. Such was the confidence reposed in Mr. Cresswell, partly on account of his ministerial office, that most Droylsden persons who had saved a few pounds, believing the investment "safe as the bank," placed them in his hands, and consequently lost their all.

Mr. Ignatius Hindley, at the commencement of the settlement, erected a warehouse on the north side of the Chapel Square, and entered into partnership with a Mr. Locke, under the firm of Locke, Hindley, and Co. Here they continued for many years to manufacture various descriptions of cotton goods on a very large scale.

Betty Hammond, the wife of Mr. Hammond, of King-street, was engaged about 1789, in part of those premises, in putting out check on commission—*i.e.*, furnishing warps and weft to the weavers, and receiving back the manufactured goods when finished.

John Travis, about 1794, and until his failure, subsequent to 1807, manufactured muslin, check, gingham, and nankeen, in the building of four storeys, inclusive of basement (lately used as the Temperance Room), and erected for him as a warehouse by his father-in-law, Robert Booth.

William Howarth, of Greenside, manufactured checks to a slight extent; and, afterwards purchasing the premises in King-street from Mr. Hammond, his two sons, John and

Benjamin Howarth, began to manufacture goods there. The former hung himself in the warehouse, and the latter became insane.

Benjamin Howarth, of Greenside, in addition to bleaching, manufactured check during the five closing years of last century.

Peter Halley, in his younger days, manufactured nankeen in the Brethren's House, afterwards at Seventhorns' Wells, and lastly, about 1800, in the warehouse in Edge-lane.

The "Sisters" commenced putting out muslins for hand loom weaving, very early after spinning was discontinued in Fairfield, perhaps about 1796. The goods so made were chiefly used by themselves in their fancy needlework ; and the practice, it appears, was only continued until the material was exhausted which had been left from their spinning.

Mr. William Hopwood, about 1797, erected a large house in Edge-lane, with the intention of applying for a licence to open it as a public-house ; but he was drowned in the canal lock close by. Subsequently, Mr. Lawrence Hall finished and converted the building into a warehouse, and commenced the manufacture of common check, and took in as partner William Gillibrand, of Droylsden, who had previously put out for John Travis. After their dissolution, Hall removed into Openshaw, and Gillibrand engaged with Haigh, Marshall, and Tidswell, of Manchester. Peter Halley manufactured nankeen here, about 1800, for a short time ; then, after standing empty awhile, the building was taken down.

Abel Tomlinson, in 1802, and several years later, on commission, manufactured muslins, cambrics, &c., in Little Droylsden. With the rest of the trade, he once made an abatement of 42s. per warp, at one blow.

Mr. John Lees, jun., who learned the business with Locke, Hindley, and Co., about 1813, put out weaving in the premises now occupied by Mr. Hines, butcher. Mr. Lees was engaged in the banking business ; and, in 1824, erected at his own cost the Moravian Chapel and Schools at Salem, near Oldham.

Mr. John Hindley, son of Mr. James Hindley, putter out

for the firm in which his brother was a partner, also, on commission, put out hand loom weaving in part of the premises occupied by the single men. Mr. Joshua Warren afterwards superintended a concern for hand loom weavers in the same place.

Mr. William Linney came from Crossgate, Audenshaw, to reside in King-street, Droylsden, about 1816, and commenced the manufacture of muslins and other goods in the premises previously occupied by John Travis, where he continued till his death several years after.

Mr. William Rothwell, in the beginning of 1833, began to manufacture, in Fairfield, on his own account, all descriptions of trimmings for hats, lutestrings, and persians, besides putting out cotton weaving, such as handkerchiefs, checks, and ginghams, for Mr. Thomas Johnson, of Manchester. Together they employed about fifty weavers in Droylsden and its vicinity; and Rothwell, dying in 1835, his widow continued putting out for several years.

Most of the early concerns failed at last. The father of one of the parties remarked to his son that he could keep him as a gentleman with £500 per annum, but he could not maintain him as a manufacturer.

During the closing ten or fifteen years of last century, there were engaged in hand loom weaving from thirty to forty persons in Fairfield alone, and a still larger number in the rest of the township, the majority of dwelling houses having a loom shop attached. The number or scale of employers was disproportioned, and consequently many of the weavers sought work elsewhere. The principal masters in the neighbourhood were—Slater, of Woodhouses; Irwin, of Newton Heath; Philips and Jackson, and Rushforth, of Manchester; Thomas Knight, of Crowcroft, Kirkmanshulme; Richard Whitehead, William Ashton, Robert Grimshaw, George Grimshaw, Thomas Sidebotham, and George Shawcross, of Gorton; George Taylor, of Openshaw; John Grimshaw, William Walker, William Linney, and Bentley and Wilkinson, of Audenshaw; Chadwicks, of Currier Lane; Lewes, of Ryecroft; John Orrell, John Gartside, and Redfern, of Ashton-under-Lyne.

About 1795, a considerable quantity of fancy goods was made—spotted shawls and handkerchiefs, and also spotted muslin—which after being woven was placed in a frame something like the twisting-in frame used in cotton mills; the spotted surface was placed upwards and the lower one was then cut by a pair of scissors bent for the purpose. This gave employment to many females; but care was necessary lest the cloth should be cut through. The patterns were various, and our grandmothers in these "fair white gowns looked wondrous fine." This method of weaving fancy work was superseded first by the "drawboy," which consisted of a number of handles, perhaps thirty or forty, attached to stout cards, and hanging by the side of the loom. A boy (hence the name) first pulled one, and then another, thus lifting up the shafts, or rather the healds, whilst the weaver made use of the treadles to pull the ground down to make room for the shuttle. Subsequently the handles were removed, and strong cords, answering the same purpose, were placed at the side of the loom. Some improvement was made by the "dobbin," and also by the "witch," and finally by the "jacquard."

A few facts may not be out of place relative to wages in "the days of prosperity," about the commencement of the century, when hand loom weaving had attained its meridian. Seventeen shillings a cut were paid in 1804 for weaving shirtings 24 yards long, 40 inches wide, made in a 72 reed, with 20 picks to the quarter inch; whilst cloth of a similar texture, or nearly so, and 25 yards long, is now woven at the mills for 1s. per cut!

Although various kinds of goods were manufactured at that time, yet the principal was gingham, chiefly in a 90 reed, but ranging from 60 to 120, the weaving of which was remunerated at one shuttle, 1s.; two shuttles, 1s. 1d.; and three shuttles, 1s. 2d. per yard. Two or three years later, Messrs. Bentley and Wilkinson paid for weaving the same material, cuts 24 yards long, 9-8ths wide, 90 reed, 30 picks to the quarter, 23s. for striped, and 23s. 6d. for chequered; whilst Messrs. Locke, Hindley, and Co., paid 26s. for a superior article.

Other sorts of work were hair cords, cambric, muslin, and jaconet. The late Mr. James Bowker wove, it is believed, the finest muslin ever manufactured in this country. It was intended for cambric hankerchiefs, was 38 inches wide, in a 160 reed, 40 picks to the quarter inch, and the price paid for weaving by Mr. Woodcroft, of New Cannon-street, Manchester, was 2s. each. Mr. Lewis, of Ryecroft, also paid 2s. per yard for 54 inches wide, and 35 picks per quarter.

Such was the demand for goods at that time, and up to 1812, or two or three years later, that no weaver, however unskilful as a workmen, need be without employment, and masters competed, not, as at present, which should get his work done at the lowest rate, but which should give the highest remuneration for labour. A strife arose in this respect between Mr. John Orrell, of Ashton, who afterwards erected, and occupied till his death, the extensive cotton mill in Openshaw, and the above mentioned Mr. Lewis, each trying to exceed the other in high wages. Eventually the contest was gained by Mr. Orrell, when his weavers subscribed and presented him with a silver cup to commemorate the event.

About that period the Droylsden weavers to Messrs. Bentley and Wilkinson, of Audenshaw, are said to have played and amused themselves as best they could on Mondays and Tuesdays, joined in country dances on the wooden turnbridge in Green-lane during Wednesday, and then on the last three days "worked like mad," in order to get in their work before Saturday at noon. Good hands even in that space of time could earn from 20s. to 23s., though it must be admitted that, after once starting, they knew little intermission till the close of the week.

Those, says Mr. Bowker, were indeed halcyon days, when workmen could stay at their homes, earn a good living, and occasionally take a day's pleasure or two, without feeling any embarrassing effects therefrom. Masters frequently came to seek weavers, liberally treated them with liquor, and concocted many ingenious plans, in order to induce them to change employers. And it is a fact that weavers took out work from as many as three or four masters at a time, weaving first a little for one and then for another. And it is a lamentable fact that few, very few, profited by that prosperity, for many were poor, very poor, at that time. Perhaps the mark will not be overshot in asserting that about one out of every hundred made a good use of those golden opportunities, which, after a few years, passed away, alas! never more to return.

In 1816, or the year after, came the downfall of gingham. The price for weaving 90 reeds, 24 yard cuts, was reduced from an average of £1 4s. to 5s. 6d. ; and in 1831, Parliament repealed the duties on printed goods, which completed the ruin of gingham and fabrics of a like nature ; and the hand loom weaver had to struggle with poverty for some years, getting any kind of work that he could. The pursuit is still slightly followed in Droylsden, but in the hamlet of Fairfield not a loom has been going for many years.

SILK AND WORSTED PLUSH WEAVING.

Mr. Samuel Travis, son of the John Travis before named, about 1812 or 1813, introduced the weaving of silk plush for hats, but so difficult was it found to be, that for some years very few could be found to overcome it. Ultimately, however, the weavers got the upper hand, and drove briskly on ; and when Mr. Travis could not furnish them with warps, he allowed them 2s. a day for playing! In the course of a few years other masters began, viz. Messrs. Todd and Ashworth, of Newton Heath ; James Hyde, of Gorton; Mrs. Bissett, and Hoyle and Newbury, of Manchester ; the latter, about the year 1835, putting out silk plush and worsted at Fairfield.

For some years at first, wages kept good; but, alas! there shortly came a fall from about 4s. 6d. per yard, the highest rate given by Mr. Travis, to about 2s. or 1s. 6d. This resulted from the French exporting so much silk plush to this country.

The only persons at present engaged in this trade in Droylsden are, Mr. Joseph Howarth, of Greenside, worsted plush; Mr. William Baguley, of Market-street, and Mr. Richard Wharmby, of Castle, silk plush manufacturers.

THE MODERN COTTON TRADE.

Before briefly noticing each concern, it may be as well to give a few general observations. The mills and sheds are destitute of architectural display, and may curtly be described as huge, oblong, utilitarian erections of brick and mortar, enclustered with numerous subsidiary buildings, and distinguished by an elevated octagonal chimney. The steam engines dispensing motion in these industrial hives comprise, in the aggregate, as ascertained from an actual return in April last, 665 nominal, or upwards of 2,000 indicated horse power. There are also at work 39,114 throstle spindles, 82,504 mule spindles, and 3,184 power looms. The number of operatives employed is—males, 1,093; and females, 1,559; making a total of 2,652.

Notwithstanding the state of comparative perfection at which machinery has arrived, it is still in the course of constant improvement. Invention with utility, and progression with economy, are the watchwords of the day; hence—

> " Amidst the dust, and speed, and clamour
> Of the loom shed and the mill,
> 'Midst the clank of wheel and hammer,
> Great results are growing still."

Edge-lane Mill.—Mr. John Ollerenshaw, hat manufacturer, of Ashton-under-Lyne, on the 1st of November, 1831, purchased, for £1,625, the Edge-lane estate of twelve acres. Afterwards, his sons, under the firm of Messrs. Samuel Ollerenshaw and Brothers, commenced erecting thereon the first factory in Droylsden, wherein the powerful agency of steam was employed, and where spinning and weaving were placed under systematic mechanical control. The bed of an engine, of twenty-six horse power, was laid in 1833; and they started the first steam loom in the township on the 26th of June, the year but one following. Mr. Samuel Ollerenshaw died in August, 1844, after which the concern was carried on by his executors, until about twelve months ago, when the firm was altered to Messrs. Samuel Harrop and Co.

Fairfield Mills.—The engines first turned round in August or September, 1837; the mill got to work about the close of the year, under the firm of Messrs. W. M. Christy and Sons.

Droylsden Mills.—Messrs. Worthington, Benson, and Co., began to erect these mills about Midsummer, 1838; and in January following the structure was damaged by the great storm. Weaving was commenced on the 13th or 14th of February, 1839; throstle spinning in the ensuing May; and mule spinning shortly afterwards. The firm was changed in March, 1853, to Messrs. Ashworth, Hadwen, and Co.

Clayton Mill.—These small premises were originally built as a flax mill, by Mr. Gore, jun., and worked by an engine of eight horse power. The hands thus employed, in May, 1836, were twenty, and consisted of eight males and twelve females. Subsequently the building was owned by Mr. James Taylor, and, in 1847, as a cotton manufactory, by Mr. Silas Leigh. On his declining business, a short time since, the mill was adapted to other uses.

Clayton Weaving Shed.—This small establishment, situated near the coalpits, was erected, about twenty years ago, by Messrs. J. Leigh and Sons; and worked by them until 1856, when it was taken by Messrs. Clarke and Co.

Victoria Mills—Erected by Edmund Buckley, Esq.; the first sod being cut on the 4th of July, 1845; and cotton spinning and weaving commenced in March, 1847, by Messrs. Henry Lees and Brothers.

Angola Mill, also built by Mr. Buckley, was reared on the 14th of August, 1850, and put in full operation on the 1st of January ensuing, by Messrs. Kay, Richardson, and Wroe. In June, 1852, the latter gentleman withdrew from the firm.

Victoria Mill (Clayton).—The erection of this weaving shed was begun in the spring of 1853. The starting took place in February following, by Mr. Edward Wroe, previously alluded to, who continued to work it until July, 1857. After standing empty, the place was taken in March, 1858, by Messrs. Marland and Whitcombe, the present occupants.

———— *Mill.*—Foundations have been excavated near Droylsden Station for a new mill intended to contain en-

gines of 140 horse power; mule spindles to the number of
40,000 ; and to be worked by Messrs. J. C. and E. C. Sidebotham.

General Remarks.—The enjoyment of an abridged time
system at the mills affords extensive facilities for the cultivation of the intellect, as well as recreation of the physical
powers. In Droylsden, as elsewhere, agitation had been
long and freely at work, when, on May 1, 1848, under
authority of an act of Parliament, the hours of labour in
cotton mills and manufactories were reduced to a maximum
of ten per day. This benevolent measure was to some
extent nullified in the following March, and twelve hours
resumed by the introduction of relays of females ; but after
a trial of five months, the plan was abandoned. Frequent
had been the importunities on the part of the workpeople
for a return to shorter time, when, on August 12, 1850, the
employers commenced working their establishments sixty
hours per week, under a new act which disqualified relays
of females and young persons. A public meeting in favour
of a "genuine Ten Hours Bill" was held at the Church
Inn, March 3, 1853, and a petition embodying those views
was despatched to Parliament by the Droylsden Short Time
Committee.

Although, in 1847, in consequence of the depressed state
of trade, considerable numbers emigrated to America, yet,
owing in some measure to the energy of the millowners,
Droylsden operatives have suffered little from "short time,"
but have enjoyed almost constant and tolerably well paid
employment. And though "turn outs" have been expe-
rienced, yet the village, especially of late, has suffered
comparatively little from strikes ; * and nowhere in the
cotton district does greater sympathy exist between employers and employed than is to be met with in Droylsden.

---

* If the returns are reliable, the Droylsden operatives
contributed upwards of £700 to the "Great Strike" at
Preston.

MISCELLANEOUS TRADES.

Although Droylsden is essentially a cotton town, yet various branches of trade and manufacture have located themselves. Clayton Colliery was begun about 1790; Mr. James Brundret erected a dye works prior to 1806; and a few years previously Mr. Miller, of Fairfield, had established a copperas works, which subsequently, as well as another built adjacent by Mr. Cowley, was purchased by Edmund Buckley, Esq., of Ardwick, and their present magnitude is exemplified by the fact of their capacity to manufacture from eighty to a hundred tons of copperas per week.

In addition to a ropery, chemical works, and a patent leather manufactory, the following employ steam engines to the number stated:—Calico printing, 2; silk and cotton dyeing, 3; iron and brass founding, 1; forges, 2; copperas works, 1; alkali works, 2; boiler and gasometer, 1; farm purposes, 1; and building purposes, 1; making a total of fourteen.

According to the census of 1801, the number of persons engaged in trade, out of a population of 1,552, was 955; and in that of 1821 the families were stated at 426, and whilst 423 were returned as connected with trade, with singular inaccuracy, two only were represented as employed in agriculture. In 1831, there were 51 families chiefly engaged in agriculture; 414 in trade, manufacturers, and handicraft; and 82 variously employed, making a total of 547 families.

DIALECT, SOUBRIQUETS, ETC.

Formerly in social conversation the Christian name, if at all used, was invariably "nicked" or abbreviated. Soubriquets, from which only one or two persons in the township were exempt, were considered more requisite to distinguish folks by than either baptismal or surnames. The byname served all ordinary purposes, whilst the proper name, like the best garment, was reserved for special display in the registers of the Church at baptisms, weddings, and interments. The following are genuine specimens of the classic nomenclature once prevalent:—"Th' Owd King," "Th' Young King,"

"Duke o' York," "Stick i'th' Mud," "Owd Brush," "Owd Yure," "Owd Seawnd," "Pepper Betty," "Boggart o' Saxon," "I Fingered Thee My Gentleman," &c.

The prefix "Owd," or old, was attached to the names and soubriquets of even young persons, and was in no wise derogatory, but may be considered perhaps as a rural title of respect. Sometimes, in order to render the patronymic more euphonus to country ears, either "a," the vowel "o," contracted from "of," or "o'th'," abbreviated from "of the," was inserted between the Christian name and sur-name, as "Bob-a-Booth," "Betty-o-Ashton," and "Philip-o'th'-Hill." Three cousins bearing exactly the same patro-nymic, in order to distinguish them, were designated "Smo' Ralph," "Black Ralph," and "Stumpin' Ralph."

Shut out from much intercourse with their neighbours, the ancient vernacular of the inhabitants embraced many quaint modes of speech, expressive idioms, and peculiarities of dialect, which were anything but what is now considered standard or "gradely" English. The following *bonâ fide* colloquy is a specimen of the mother tongue of "Big Dreighlsdin," as the township was emphatically designated in days gone by. A female espies her sister, and hastening to the window, eagerly inquires, "Sally, wheeur ort gooink ?" To which Sarah responds, "Whoy, aw'm gooink o seeink iv t' buryink's commink." A few years ago Mr. H—, Lay-assistant, taking an adult to task, or, as popularly expressed, "coeink him o'er t' coals," for spiritual ignorance, met with the expostulation, "Heaw should aw know? It's ow owin' to mi breawtin's op ; aw kneaw no weeler." A local saying runs, "O' star ot top, loike owd pop Jonathan's bacon bo' brawth." A jingling rhyme, or ramble, enumerating the householders in Droylsden-lane was once in circulation ; but, like a modern doggrel of the same stamp, is irre-trievably lost. Some years back the Droylsden innkeepers were thus commemorated by the village poetaster :—

"Tummy Nick,
Charley Rick,
Billy Brew,
Sharp Shue,
Un Cappel Dick."

SECULAR EDUCATION.

According to the various MSS. and deeds on which the documentary portion of this history is based, Droylsden has not contributed more than the average number of "marksmen," and many of the signatures are by no means indifferent specimens of caligraphy. Some of the books deposited in the town's chest also exhibit penmanship in many instances tolerably well executed, and, in some cases, really good. Occasionally the orthography betrays the Lancashire or Droylsden origin of the scribe.

No account of internal efforts to promote the spread of education in the township has survived of an earlier date than the middle of last century, at which period tuition was held as an auxiliary employment, or subordinate profession. The first mention of a local preceptor occurs on February 3, 1758, when the burial of John Grundy, schoolmaster, of Droylsden, is recorded in the register of Gorton Church.

After a blank interval, in 1774, appears Jonathan Grimshaw, who, on quarterly terms, principally of one shilling and sixpence, but descending to half that amount, taught a few scholars in addition to plying the hand loom. He resided in the quaint and detached cottage in Far-lane, now occupied by Sarah Bertenshaw; and, some fifteen years later on, it is remembered that, besides a small night school, Grimshaw had about ten day pupils, some of whom sat on a form and the others on his loom rail, busy conning their tasks whilst the master was engaged weaving linen. Grimshaw, who died October 16, 1795, and was buried at Ashton Parish Church, has the honour of being the first Sunday school teacher in the township.

Sarah Hibbert, in 1775, resided near Square Fold, and taught about half a dozen tiny scholars, who, in the spare time from their few imposed lessons, picked out the seeds from cotton, preparatory to the process of slubbing, which the mistress carried on in the school.

Joseph Bertenshaw began teaching school, June 3, 1776, in Old Hill House, as appears from a memorandum in the Grimshaw obituary, or "Death Book."

A seminary for young ladies, of which Miss M. A. Willet is now governess, was commenced in Fairfield, in 1796; and an acadamy for young gentlemen, of which the Rev. William Craig is now principal, was begun about seven years afterwards.

Shortly before the close of last century, Mrs. Morris resided not far from the present King's Head, and taught about twenty small children; and "old" John Mellor, of Lane Head, in addition to his own trade, instructed families of children, and eat out his remuneration in the shape of one or two meals per week.

Early in 1802, steps were taken to erect a village school. Thomas Jones, Esq., a property owner and resident, presented an eligible site, containing 321½ square yards, situated at the south east angle of the "Little Field," and abutting on both the Droylsden and the Green-lanes. A committee was formed, and a house to house canvass instituted; the more opulent gave money, and the poorer classes labour, or money and labour conjointly. Mr. John Travis acted as treasurer, and an account of his receipts and disbursements is deposited in the town's chest. There was no formality when the foundation was laid, nor any public demonstration when the premises were completed, nor is it exactly known when they were brought into requisition. It is inferred from Mr. Travis's pecuniary statement that the building was begun on or about October 26, 1802, when, as in those days teetotalism was unknown, no less than six and three quarter gallons of gin were purchased to regale the villagers. Bricksetting operations were proverbially slow at that time, and it is not till the following November that Mr. Travis records the purchase of forms at an expense of a guinea, and the payment of six pounds to the schoolmaster, perhaps for some personal superintendence. The final item occurs on the closing day of the year, up to which period the expenditure, independently of gratuitous labour, had been £132 15s. 8d. During the next five or six years, no less than £87 18s. 5d. was disbursed from the poor rates on behalf of Droylsden school, for what purpose does not appear. Mr. Jones also subscribed five pounds towards the same object, in April, 1807, as appears by the town's books.

The edifice was a plain oblong structure of the type then current. The school measured internally 25½ feet long, by 21½ feet broad, and 13¼ feet high; and, like the cottage, was built of brick, and roofed with grey slate. A stone inserted in front of the cottage is inscribed "Droylsden School was Erected by Subscription, 1802." Entrance was obtained by a door on the southern gable, and the room was lighted by two windows on the east, and two on the west side; each window measuring 6¾ feet broad, and 5 feet high.

Several years elapsed before the site was conveyed for educational purposes. Thomas Jones, gentleman, by his indenture, dated the 21st of September, 1807, and duly enrolled in Chancery, vested it in nine trustees, and provided that, when reduced by death or resignation to a minimum of three, the survivors should fill up the vacancies by election. It is remarkable that this school is not enumerated in the Government returns of the charities in Lancashire.

Although the two first masters were successful in teaching adults on three evenings per week, and for a few years there was a tolerable attendance of day scholars, yet the institution never attained a very flourishing position. Several reasons may be assigned. No endowment was provided for the sustenance of master or mistress, and the mere free occupancy of the premises was not sufficient to induce any first class teacher to carry on the school, when his income was dependant entirely on the precarious sum to be derived from the pence of the scholars. The population, also, was too scanty and poor to furnish sufficient pupils to make it remunerative, and competition existed in the schools at Fairfield, Gorton, Audenshaw, and Crowthorn. And, in addition, the masters, generally, were not remarkable for temperance or intellectual attainments. Some of them were severe disciplinarians, and many parents preferred the village dame schools, which, assimilating to nurseries, afforded a good deal of amusement and attempted but little instruction.

Richard Bradburn, of Manchester, the first master, was appointed in 1803, and after a few months' struggle was dis-

F

charged. After a short vacancy, in the year following, John
Wilson, a resident shoemaker, was appointed to the master-
ship. Like that of his predecessor, his stay was short,
merely extending over a year or so. John Hewgill, a
Yorkshireman, but acting as exciseman at Bristol, was the
next appointment. He commenced duty about May, 1805.
One stormy night, he was bewildered in the fields, near
Water-lane, and perished; he was interred at St. Peter's,
Ashton, where the date of decease is given as January
12, 1828, and his age recorded as sixty years. Hewgill
was succeeded by his son, and previous assistant, John
Hewgill, a native of Bristol, who died suddenly, January 24,
1848, aged forty-eight years. The next appointment was
Joseph Grimshaw, a descendant of an old Droylsden family,
who, after three months' unsuccessful effort, with the consent of the trustees, obtained other employment, and resigned the tuition to his wife. The number of scholars had
diminished before the higher educational advantages offered
by the British School, until reduced to some half dozen.
Relinquishing instruction, the family left the village, 5th
August, 1857; and, on the 26th of April, in the following
year, the school was pulled down, in order to make way
for erecting the Droylsden Institute on its site.

A small private day school for boys was taught in Fairfield, by John Highland, prior to 1809 when one of a
superior kind was begun by Mr. Henry Nalty, and, with
the aid of his son, John Nalty, continued for twenty-four
years. At first Mr. Nalty used a large room, at the back of
his house (now inhabited by the Misses Lowton), but the
number of scholars became so great that he had to resort,
also, to the top room of his dwelling. Mr. Nalty survived
the discontinuance of the school for eleven years; and died
in October, 1846, at the patriarchial age of ninety-two. In
the meantime, the school had been continued, or rather re-
commenced, in the Boys' Old Sunday School, by Edward
Hollingworth; and was afterwards continued by John
Jackson, until its final relinquishment.

A day school for girls was originated about 1809, by Miss
Southall, in the house now occupied by Mr. Stewart, and

was afterwards carried on by Miss Watson in the Sisters' House, and then in the Girls' Sunday School by Miss Fox, and successively by a great number of females, including Mrs. Davies, who, since its association with the National School in 1854, has continued a small dame school in Fairfield. In June, 1854, the Moravians commenced the erection of a neat brick structure, measuring fifty feet by thirty feet internally, which was opened October 8, 1854, as a mixed day school, under the system of the National Society. And since that period, Mr. W. H. Patrick, certified master, and Miss Walker, aided by three pupil teachers, have zealously done their duty.

Mr. Alfred Andrew for several years taught a day and evening school for both sexes in premises at East End, and also instructed the short timers from Edge-lane Mill. He ceased about eight years ago, since which period Mr. Bowker has continued to teach a small mixed day school.

Various spasmodic and detached efforts have been made in the township, including those of Mr. and Miss Collins and Mr. James Rothwell in the Temperance Room, and Mr. John Ovens and others in the Independent School Room.

The earliest portion of the Queen-street School was erected by William Miller Christy, Esq., in 1838, and shortly afterwards it was opened as a juvenile and infant day school, under the superintendence of Mr. and Mrs. Buller, from the Home and Colonial Society's Training School. After their removal from the village, Miss Athowe continued the tuition on the same plan, until the close of 1843, when the mill owners resolved to extend educational operations. Mr. Christy enlarged the school at an expense of £50, and Messrs. Worthington, Benson, and Co., Samuel Ollerenshaw and Brothers, and W. M. Christy and Sons, took the premises for five years at an annual rent of £15, and agreed to make necessary internal alterations, and to cover all excess of expenditure over the children's pence by a rate, to be assessed half on the spinning, and half on the weaving (based on the number of looms and spindles) in each concern. Accordingly, on January 16, 1844, the school was

F 2

reopened by Mr. Samuel Dawson and Miss Athowe, the
former teaching the juveniles under the system of the
British and Foreign School Society, and the latter the
infants on the previous system. The school was placed
under Government in August, 1848. After Miss Athowe's
vacation, the industrial superintendence over the female
department was undertaken first by Miss Collins, then by
her sister, and since by Mrs. Dawson. Mr. Christy erected,
at right angles with the original building, a handsome and
commodious school room of red and white brick, roofed with
slates of two colours, in alternate stripes. The interior,
which is open to the roof, and lighted by skylights, each
consisting of a single square, measures fifty-four feet long,
twenty-six feet broad, and twenty-four feet to the ridge.
The opening took place April 25, 1851, with the annual
public examination of the pupils. There are now in these
flourishing and well conducted schools nine pupil teachers
in the juvenile department under Mr. Dawson, and four in
the infants' school, which is presided over by Miss Annabella
Ferguson, from the Glasgow Training College, who was
appointed mistress in April, 1851.

Messrs. Wood and Wright, of Bankbridge, since January
8, 1855, have provided an excellent teacher, Mr. James
Swallow, for the instruction of their young workpeople,
and others choosing to attend. Clayton Episcopal Day
School was opened March 9, 1857. Mr. Morris teaches in
the school room at Edge-lane; and the Roman Catholic
children generally attend their day school in Openshaw.

LITERARY, EDUCATIONAL, AND SCIENTIFIC INSTITUTIONS.

The earliest association of this nature known to have been
instituted in the township was the Botanical Society, in
Little Droylsden, which is noticed more fully elsewhere.

A Young Men's Mutual Improvement Society was begun
in the winter of 1839-40 by James Turner and half a dozen
associates, who met in the front room of a dwelling house in
Market-street, now occupied by Mr. Bullock. The range
of instruction included reading, writing, arithmetic, geography, grammar, and debate, whilst a newspaper and

several periodicals were provided. The highest number of members attained was about forty, and three times the society removed to more eligible premises, until, after an existence of three seasons, it became extinct.

A small Chemical Society was started, about 1841, in the cellar beneath the shop in Market-street now kept by Mr. Shepherd. In this humble laboratory and meeting room, the members studied the rudiments of chemistry, and manufactured blacking and furniture paste, which were sold to defray expenses. After a brief career, the society was dissolved.

The Fairfield and Droylsden Naturalists' Society was founded in February, 1842, by Mr. J. W. Slater, in conjunction with George Hill, of Durham-street. Its original aim was limited to promoting the study of natural history. The first place of meeting was an upper room in the house now occupied by Mr. James Bowker, in Fairfield, from whence in about ten months' time, owing to the want of accommodation, they removed to a loft in the house occupied by William Entwistle, adjoining the site of the present Educational Institute. The objects of the society were at first misunderstood. Many suspected they were political or theological, and the owner of the house wrote to his tenant, who was also a member of the society, warning him to "stop the meetings"; and, in consequence, another removal took place to a house near the corner of Greenside-lane. At this place, the first exhibition, chiefly of objects of natural history, was held in the wakes week of the same year. About this period, it was found that the society required, in a village like Droylsden, a broader basis than the study of the natural sciences alone afforded, and some elementary classes were commenced. At the first annual soirée, held in the Wesleyan Chapel, in 1843, amongst others, the late celebrated electrician, W. Sturgeon, was present. The members increasing, the society removed to Lane End, and on January 23, 1845, altered its designation to the Fairfield and Droylsden Naturalists' Society and Mechanics' Institute, afterwards to Fairfield and Droylsden Mechanics' Institute, and lastly, on March 24, 1851, the term was restricted to

Droylsden Mechanics' Institution. The society was flourishing and useful from 1843 to 1847, and also had the honour
of being one of the first to join the Lancashire and Cheshire
Institutional Union ; and for two years Mr. J. W. Slater, as
its president, was elected a member of the central committee
of the union.

The Young Men's Society (or Association) in connection
with St. Mary's Church Sunday School, was founded in
January, 1848, for the acquirement of Christian knowledge
and the cultivation of general learning. Under the management of a committee of seven, including president, vice-
president, treasurer, and secretary, and, with the exception
of the permanent president (Rev. P. Thompson, B.A.), all
annually elected, the society met four or five nights a week
during the season. The number of members fluctuated ; the
the highest was in November, 1852, when there were seven
honorary, thirty-eight general, and five females making a
total of fifty members. Information was imparted by means
of elementary classes, lectures, discussions, and the perusal
of newspapers and magazines. The association effected
considerable good in a quiet, unostentatious way ; and
acquired a useful collection of books, once designed as the
nucleus of a village library.

A Mutual Improvement Class was existing in connection with the Independent Sunday School, in October,
1849 ; but it subsequently fell into desuetude. A successor,
bearing a similar title, was established January 1, 1854, and
held meetings in the school room for the discussion of
questions, the reading of essays, and delivery of lectures,
for the moral and intellectual improvement of members,
and to facilitate acquaintance and fellowship with individuals of similar views and character. During its existence, thirty-six members at different times belonged to the
society.

The Emulation Society, in connection with St. Ann's
Roman Catholic Chapel, Seventhorns' Wells—a step in the
right direction—was commenced August 4, 1850, but only
existed a short time.

The Droylsden Literary Society, for the reading of

original compositions, &c., was begun on the 9th of April, 1855, but after a few bi-monthly meetings, commencing on the 7th of the following May, the society became defunct.

General Remarks.—Apparently during the last sixty or seventy years the township has never been destitute of a night school, of some sort or other, for the improvement of young men. Special, but short lived, and not continuous, efforts in this respect have been made for the benefit of young women. Many years ago, the managers of the Fairfield Sunday School attempted by week day evening instruction to improve the intellectual attainments of females whose education had been neglected. Subsequently, the cause was embarked in by the Wesleyan Sunday School, then by the Church Sunday School, next by Mrs. Benson in the Independent School Room, afterwards by the Mechanics' Institution, and since by the Educational Institution.

The Mechanics' Institution, the Young Men's Association, and the Mutual Improvement Class, for some time simultaneously sustained the common object of imparting knowledge to all who desired partially to retrieve the neglect of earlier years. At length, after several conferences of delegates with a view to promote increased usefulness and efficiency, on March 31, 1857, the three societies were amalgamated under the title of the Droylsden Educational Institution. The premises lately held by the Mechanics' Institution proved totally inadequate to the growing requirements of the new society, and four distinct suites of apartments had to be engaged for the use of the classes.

After an application from the directors, the trustees of the old school united with them, and, in conjunction with a few others, constituted a committee for collecting subscriptions, and appointed an executive for procuring plans and estimates, and for superintending the new building. Ultimately, through the liberality of friends and neighbours, the former unsightly school room was replaced by the present edifice, the foundation stone of which was unosten-

tatiously laid, June 5, 1858, by Richard Christy, Esq.,
chairman of the Building Committee.

THE DROYLSDEN INSTITUTE.

This elegant and attractive building, which stands on
the site of the old Day School, at the bisection of Market-
street by the Ashton New-road, proves useful to the inhabitants, as well as a graceful ornament to the centre of the
village. It is built in the Gothic style, from the designs of
Mr. Alfred Waterhouse, architect, of Manchester, who also
superintended the erection, the contractors being Messrs.
Thomas Bates and Co., of Droylsden. The edifice is a
rectangular structure, faced externally with the local red
stock bricks, relieved with stone dressings and fire brick
bands, and stands on a basement of stone. The white bricks
are also introduced alternately with the red ones in the
arches over the windows. Above the eastern entrance is inscribed "Droylsden Institute," and on worked stone labels in
the gable adjoining, " Erected by voluntary contributions,"
with the date, " 1858," in a monogram on an oval medallion
in the centre. There are two storeys to the building. On
the ground floor the window openings are four feet wide; on
the upper floor they are smaller, and arranged in groups of
three. The roof is acute in pitch, covered with alternate
stripes of blue and green slates, and on the south receives a
broken and varied outline from the chimney stacks at the
ends, the octagonal ventilating turret in the centre of
the ridge, and a range of five dormer windows. The
interior is commodious and well adapted for educational
purposes. On the ground floor, to the left of the entrance
lobby from the south, or principal front, is the library, used
also as a committee room and a class room, lighted by a
triplet window, and occupied by the females. On the
opposite side is a convenient and well furnished news room,
measuring 28 feet by 18 feet, fitted up with tables, &c., of
pitch pine; and beyond are two class rooms, supplied with
desks and other requisites for the male members.

The whole of the upper storey forms a spacious hall, 60
feet by 28 feet, and 31 feet 6 inches high; is used for

Droylsden Educational Institute.

lectures, concerts, and public assemblies; and has a permanent, raised, and graduated platform at one end, to which a separate staircase from the library affords private access from below. The roof, of five bays, is plastered, and supported by stained deal principals; and being of high pitch, imparts a lofty appearance to the room. The hall is heated by a stove; ventilated in the roof, on Mim's four point system; and lighted by seven window groupings on the south and east sides, by the dormer windows above, and, at a corresponding height, by a sixfoil, or rose window, at each end. The entrance to this room is from Market-street, by a stone staircase, with closets beneath, and a small anteroom on the top, level with the public hall, and furnished with apparatus necessary for tea meetings, &c.

The old cottage dwelling was left standing, and is now occupied by the warden or keeper of the premises. In the *Illustrated London News*, of the 2nd of February last, appeared a description of the building, together with a wood cut, from which the accompanying illustration is derived by an electrotype cast.

The original estimate for erecting the new edifice was £750, but the contract was enhanced by extra excavations on the eastern side, by widening the building four feet, and other alterations. These, together with fixtures and furniture, including fire ranges, gas fittings, platform, palisading, and the architect's fee, raised the total cost to £1,199 6s. 2½d. of which £674 5s. 9d. has been subscribed, leaving a debt of £525 0s. 5½d., for which the trustees are personally responsible. At one period, hopes were entertained that an educational grant from Government would have been available in assisting to reduce the debt, but a lengthy correspondence resulted in disappointment. The mixed character of the objects to which the building was intended to be devoted removed it from within the scope of Government allowances.

The ceremony of inauguration extended over two days. Saturday, November 20, 1858, was devoted to a procession, tea party, and concert; and the Monday following to a public meeting. On the Saturday afternoon, the village was the scene of unwonted festivity and rejoicing; banners and flags being displayed from the mills, workshops, dwellings, and across the streets. A large and well organised procession, consisting of several bands of music, the trustees, Building Committee, directors, members, and friends of the Educational Institution, and the members of various friendly societies, in their holiday paraphernalia, moved from the Recreation Grounds, round by Edge-lane and Fairfield, and terminated at the new building. Richard Christy, Esq., chairman of the Building Committee, and secretary to the trustees, then declared the institute to be publicly opened, after which 660 persons took tea in the large room, which was tastefully decorated. The remainder of the evening was devoted to a vocal and instrumental concert.

The meeting on Monday was presided over by the Right Rev. the Lord Bishop of Manchester. The room was crowded, not less than 700 persons being present; and the platform was well filled with ministers and gentlemen from various places. After the report of the Building Committee had been read by Joseph Hadwen, Esq., honorary secretary, the right rev. chairman delivered a most excellent address, and speeches were afterwards given by Thomas Bazley, Esq., M.P.; Ivie Mackie, Esq., mayor of Manchester; Malcolm Ross, Esq.; Rev. James Bardsley, M.A.; Edmund Potter, Esq.; Henry Ashworth, Esq.; William Tipping, Esq. (Kent); Rev. P. Thompson, B.A.; and Richard Christy, Esq.

The premises remain in the hands of trustees, and, in fulfilment of the requirements of the original trust, a portion, including the lecture hall and two class rooms, is used, during the day time only, as an extension of the British School. In the evening, the reserved part, together with the news room, library, and female class room at all times, is occupied entirely by the directors of the Educational Institution for the purpose of instructing the members in the various branches of a liberal and useful education. By an arrangement made at a meeting of the members held on the 7th of last December, the directors, on obtaining possession of the building, were authorised to pay a rent equivalent to the interest on the money borrowed, the rent to diminish proportionately with the reduction of the debt, and to cease altogether with its liquidation.

From the second annual report of the directors in February last, it appeared that the income of the year had been £82 6s. 3½d., and the expenditure £73 11s. 6d., which left £8 14s. 9½d. as a balance in hand. The names on the books comprised—Males, honorary members, 13; adults, 151; juveniles, 50 : and females, 40 : total, 254 : or, exclusive of Clayton, which furnishes no members, about one in every 23 of the population of the township. The subjects studied in the classes included arithmetic, geometry, and algebra, writing and mechanical drawing, reading, dictation, and elocution, English history, geography, and the French language. The news room was supplied with one or more copies of one quarterly, five monthly, fifteen weekly, and two daily newspapers, serials, and magazines.

This institution, under vigorous management, by administering to the mental and intellectual requirements of such as choose to avail themselves of its privileges, and by otherwise advancing literary, scientific, and useful knowledge, is capable of doing much in ameliorating the social condition of the village.

THE CHURCH OF ENGLAND.

Droylsden, no doubt, in its ecclesiastical relationship was tributary to Manchester Parish Church from the time of its foundation. The first authentic information respecting this association occurs in the grant in 1422 of its tythes towards the endowment of the Collegiate Church. The villagers were dependent on the clergy of that church for the little spiritual supervision they obtained, and there they took part in baptism, confirmation, marriage, and interment. For the latter purpose, a place called "Droylsden Hill" was reserved on the south side of the Collegiate Church, and retained its appellation so late as 1680. One of the Cathedral sidesmen, annually elected, is still chosen out of Droylsden. Probably, on the erection at Ashton of a chapel of ease, which was existing in the thirteenth century, some of the Droylsdenians, from its proximity, resorted thither.

In connection with the township the first notice of the Established Church, prior to the Reformation, is in 1400, when the Bishop of Lichfield and Coventry granted a licence to Sir John Byron to have an oratory for one year in his manors of Clayton and Butterworth; and, eleven years afterwards, the licence was renewed and extended "throughout his manors in Lancashire." After this, both history and tradition are silent for centuries. The oratory being intended for the exclusive use of the Byron family, their servants and tenantry, it did not require episcopal consecration. It seems questionable whether the service of the Protestant Church of England was ever celebrated in its precincts. The Byrons, on the spoliation of the abbeys and monasteries, in 1540, obtained a grant of Newstead Abbey, in Nottinghamshire, and deserted Clayton Hall. Probably the tenant, unable to maintain a private chaplain, would resort to the public ministry at Gorton, or Newton Heath, and the oratory would be disused. Apparently the two latter chapels were existing prior to the Reformation; and the Byrons, and subsequently the Chethams, possessed lofts, or galleries, in both; and Humphrey Chetham, when at Clayton, is traditionally affirmed to have worshipped in the former. Towards the close of the Commonwealth era, but never subsequent to the passing of the Act of Uniformity, baptismal rites—Presbyterian of course—are recorded in Gorton Church register as having been celebrated at Clayton Hall, and most likely in the domestic chapel.

Doubtless, on the erection of a chapel of ease at Newton, first mentioned in 1573, Droylsden, for ecclesiastical purposes, was considered to be comprised within that reputed chapelry. Probably no formal assignment to Newton ever took place, any more than to Gorton or Ashton, the caprice or convenience of the population constituting the only rule recognised; for some of the estates, as Clayton Hall and the (South) Clockhouse, possessed forms or seats in the chapels both at Newton and Gorton. The inhabitants of Greenside, owing to proximity, habitually or occasionally

resorted to Newton; those on the southerly side frequented
Gorton; and the easterly portion usually attended Ashton;
consequently, the baptisms, marriages, and interments were
divided. The Parliamentary Commissioners, of June, 1650,
report that Droylsden is nearer to the chapel of Newton
than any other township, and that the inhabitants make use
of the same. They also recommend that Droylsden, and
several hamlets adjacent to Newton, should be united, and
formed into a parish, and connected with Newton Chapel.
In the early part of the last century, about 1717, Bishop
Gaskell, in his notes respecting Newton Chapel, observes
that to that chapelry belong the township of Newton and
Failsworth, and *part* of Moston, Droylsden, and Bradford.
Although there only partially assigned to Newton, and reasons
exist for supposing the remainder prescriptively appertained
to Gorton; yet, when these real or supposed ancient bonds
of union were dissevered, and Droylsden was formed into
a "Peelite" parish, the incumbent of Newton, claiming the
sole jurisdiction, obtained from the Ecclesiastical Commissioners an annual grant for the supposed loss of his fees.
In 1673, and doubtless long before, Newton annually elected
two chapelwardens. In the reign of George I., according
to Gaskell, that for Newton was chosen by the minister,
and the other, for Failsworth, by the chapelry, every third
year, out of Moston and Droylsden, according to canon.
For the use of Droylsden's town officials, four mahogany
staves, silver capped, and inscribed, " *Georgius IV. Britt.
Rex Fid. Def.* 1821," were purchased by the ratepayers, and
lodged in Newton Church. These staves now grace the
pew of the wardens in Droylsden Church.

Newton Episcopal Chapel fell down on the 2nd of May,
1808, and remained in ruins for six years. The cost of
re-erection was defrayed by a rate, levied under authority
of two several acts of Parliament, 54 and 57 Geo. III.,
empowering the wardens to levy rates on all rateable property in the townships of Newton, Failsworth, Moston, and
Droylsden. This was a landlord's tax, amounting to something like four per cent. on the rental, and was collected for
many years, longer, perhaps, than was necessary.

The spiritual destitution of the place continued to augment, so far as the Church was concerned, with the increase of population, until January 19, 1840, when the Rev. William Hutchinson, incumbent of Newton Heath, having obtained the sanction of the bishop of the diocese and the consent of the trustees, issued an address to the inhabitants of Droylsden, and, in conjunction with the Rev. John Whitley, M.A., incumbent of Openshaw, commenced on the following Sabbath an afternoon service in the old school, since replaced by the new Institute. These clergymen preached alternately, and their ministry was attended by a number of persons; but no Sabbath school was established, and the enterprise was shortly afterwards abondoned.

After a further interval of about four years, the Churchmen of the township began to bestir themselves. At a meeting held on April 2, 1844, consisting of Robert Benson, Esq., Samuel Ollerenshaw, Esq., and Mr. John Hewgill, the names of twenty-six persons were announced, who, in the aggregate, offered to subscribe £622 6s. in aid of funds for the erection of a new church. On the 22nd of the following October, Droylsden was severed from the spiritual authority of Newton; and, under the judicious act of Sir Robert Peel (6th and 7th Vic. c. 37), for the extension of church accommodation in populous places, was formed into a separate and distinct parish for ecclesiastical purposes. In the ensuing December, the Rev. Philip Thompson, B.A., of St. Catharine's Hall, Cambridge, and curate of Christ Church, Macclesfield, was nominated by the Crown to the incumbency of the new district. Mr. Thompson commenced his residence in January, 1845, and issued an address to his parishioners on the 4th of the following month. Having obtained from the Bishop of Chester a licence for the Queen-street School Room, the use of which had been granted by Messrs. W. M. Christy and Sons, Messrs. Worthington, Benson, and Co., and Messrs. Samuel Ollerenshaw and Brothers, on February 9, 1845, he commenced divine service therein, and opened a Sunday school in the same premises exactly a month afterwards. The congregation increasing, an agitation for the erection of a church was renewed; and the object was finally

accomplished by individual subscription, aided by grants of
£500 from the Ecclesiastical Commissioners for Building
Churches, £500 from the Incorporated Society for Building
Churches and Chapels, £500 from the Chester Diocesan Society, and £150 from a fund placed by Sir R. Peel in the hands
of the Ecclesiastical Commissioners for the purposes of church
extension. The site of the church is immediately contiguous to the Ashton New-road, near the eastern extremity of
the township, and with the graveyard contains 4,225 superficial square yards of land, presented by the late P. R. Hoare,
Esq., banker, of London, one of the co-heirs of the Clayton
estate. The foundation stone of the church was laid on the
wake Tuesday, August 25, 1846, by Robert Benson, Esq., of
Fairfield, amidst great public rejoicing, a procession, tea
meeting, and other demonstrations celebrating the event.

After an unavoidable delay, consequent on the creation of
the see of Manchester, the edifice was dedicated to Saint
Mary, on February 11, 1848, by Dr. Lee, the Right Rev.
Lord Bishop of Manchester, and this constituted his first
official act in the diocese. The sermon was preached from
Leviticus xix. 30, by the Very Rev. the Dean of Manchester. The structure, which is in the early English style
of Gothic architecture, was designed by Mr. E. H. Shellard,
architect, of Manchester; and Messrs. Haworth, of Todmor-
den, contracted for the masons' work, and Messrs. Coulthurst
and Froggat, of Cheetham Hill, for the carpenters' work and
the remainder of the building. The total cost was upwards
of £3,500, and a debt of £1,000, left due to the Building
Committee, was paid off about four years afterwards by
those who were liable.

The edifice is built of Yorkshire stone, commonly designated "perepoints," in random courses, with dressed ashlar quoins to the windows, and intervening buttresses. The
nave is 76 feet 8 inches long by 22 feet 3 inches wide, the
north and south aisles each 74 feet by 10 feet 6 inches, and
the spacious chancel measures 37 feet 6 inches by 18 feet.
The vestry is placed in the angle formed by the chancel and
north aisle, and contains on the basement storey a steam
boiler and apparatus requisite for heating the church. The

western front of the church, which is striking and impressive,
is embellished with an enriched door in the central compart-
ment, surmounted by a window of two lights with trefoil
heads, and a quatrefoil above, enclosed in an arch, over
which is a small ventilating light corresponding with one in
the eastern gable. On the apex above, an ornamental bell cot
temporarily supplies the place of an appropriate tower and
spire to be placed in the south west angle. The roof, which
is of a very high pitch, is covered with green Westmoreland
slates, with ridge tiles on the summit. The eastern apices
of the nave and chancel, and also the apex of the porch, are
terminated with floriated crosses. There are two entrances
to the church, a door at the west end, and a handsome porch
abutting against the south side of the south aisle. The
entrance for the clergy to the chancel is closed externally,
but that to the vestry is open. The interior is chaste and
ecclesiastical, though devoid of decoration. The only attempt yet made—at the expense of a lady, a member of the
congregation—is the sculpture of the north corbel of the
chancel arch to represent the head of Cranmer, the martyr,
and the corresponding one on the south that of Ridley.
Above the arch the invitation, " Oh ! come let us worship,"
is suitably inscribed. Within the chancel, pews have been
constructed, and the creed and decalogue appear in church
text; but the sedilia remains in an unfinished state. On
the south side, a plain cenotaph, of black and statuary
marble, briefly commemorates "Elizabeth Midwood, of
Huddersfield, who died at Fairfield, June 5, 1856, aged
62 years." The whole of the roofs are framed in open
timber work after the ancient fashion, the boarded ceiling
stained in imitation of old English oak ; the tie beams, by
which the roof of the nave is supported, being themselves
supported by wall pieces and braces resting on unsculptured
corbels. The nave is separated from the aisles by two rows
of handsome, polished, and clustered shafts, forming on each
side a light arcade with carved capitals, and five moulded
and pointed arches, supporting a lofty clerestory, lighted by
trefoil windows, alternately lancet shaped and semi-circular.

Light is also admitted by means of six couplet windows

in the north, and five in the south aisle, and another in its
gable, and two (both lancet shaped) at the west end. The
chancel has three lanceolated windows, with trefoil heads,
on the south side, and two on the north, and an enriched
triplet at the east end. At present there is no stained glass.
All the openings are leaded, and glazed with lozenge
quarrels, and, excepting the clerestory, are of a greenish
yellow tinted glass.

The west end is occupied by a small gallery, which
affords accommodation for a part of the school children and
also the choir, and a well toned organ, which was opened
May 12, 1855, and completed and gilded last year, at a
total cost of nearly £300. The pews are framed in the
olden style, with *fleur de lis* finials, stained in imitation of
oak. Accommodation is afforded for 800 persons, including
541 free sittings by open seats. The pulpit, sculptured in
white Roche Abbey stone, was originally approached from
the vestry by means of a staircase in the wall, but has been
removed to the north side of the chancel arch, whilst the
reading desk, somewhat elaborate, is placed on the opposite
side. The font is of stone, and stands upon two steps,
adjacent to the south or principal entrance. It is an exact
copy of a very ancient font, dated 1400, in All Saints',
Leicester. The bowl is ornamented with foliage, flowers,
fruits, and heads, and corbels resting on shafts attached to
a round stem. The church was fitted up with gas on the
3rd of November, 1852, when service in the afternoon was
superseded by that in the evening.

The living is an incumbency and rectory, endowed by
the Ecclesiastical Commissioners with £150 per annum,
which, with seat rents, surplice fees, &c., enhance the value
to £250, as returned to the Pastoral Aid Society. Unfortunately, as yet, it is destitute of a *domus parochiæ*. On the
erection of Droylsden Church, the Rev. W Hutchinson,
incumbent of Newton Heath, received an annual grant of
£15 from the Ecclesiastical Commissioners for the supposed
loss of fees. The parish registers commence as follows:—
Baptisms, March, 1845; burials, February, 1848; and marriages in the June following. The rite of baptism is

administered only on the first Sabbath in the month, at a special service, and immediately after the second lesson, catechetical examination of the scholars supplying the place of a sermon. The graveyard is enclosed by a neat stone wall, with handsome entrance gates on the south and west, and is planted with a line of thriving trees on every side except the north. In addition to flat grave stones, a few upright memorials have been erected, including a chaste floriated cross to the memory of Thomas Henry, son of the Rev. Philip Thompson, who died February 6, 1857, aged five years.

THE FIRST SUNDAY SCHOOL.

Sunday school instruction was introduced into Droylsden by Jonathan Grimshaw, of Far-lane, and James Booth, of the White Hart. For that purpose Mr. Booth liberally granted the use of the second floor of the three storeyed building adjacent to the public-house, which was erected by him as a spinning room a year or two previously, and was then in his own occupation as a provision shop. The room, which still retains the appellation of the " school chamber," was entered externally by means of a flight of steps abutting on the gable. These were subsequently removed, and the lower part of the doorway filled up with brickwork, whilst in the upper portion a casemented window was inserted.

The duration of the school is ascertained, from a record of the teacher, to have extended over 120 Sundays, from the 28th of January, 1787, to the 17th of May, 1789, inclusive. The teacher seems to have received from Booth a remuneration of £9, or at the rate of 1s. 6d. per Sabbath. A Bible, still preserved, contains in his handwriting the inscription—" Sunday School, Jonathan Grimshaw, July 10th day, 1788." The room on the Sabbath was used exclusively for teaching the scholars, who numbered from twenty to thirty; the instruction was entirely of a secular nature, and the reason of the school's discontinuance is no longer remembered.

CHURCH SUNDAY SCHOOL.

Soon after the erection of the village day school, now replaced by the Droylsden Institute, in or about 1803, John Swindells, senior, of Green Lane, obtained permission from the trustees to commence a Sabbath school therein. With Swindells were associated Henry Holland, Thomas and George Selby (brothers), and John and Jonathan Grimshaw, sons of the first Sunday school teachers in Droylsden. A collection was made in the neighbourhood wherewith to purchase the first supply of copy books and other materials requisite for reading and writing, then included in Sabbath school instruction. The catechism of the Church of England was also taught to the scholars. This undertaking continued but a few years through Bradburn's short mastership of the day school, and until his successor, Wilson, conceiving it interfered with his interest and vocation, complained to the trustees, at whose request the school was unwillingly relinquished.

An interval of more than forty years elapsed ere the Church resumed the Sabbath school instruction of the young. The Rev. P. Thompson, B.A., on the 9th of March, 1845, commenced a Church Sunday school in the Queen-street School Room, then recently opened by him for divine service. The teachers on the first Sabbath included James Schofield, James Rothwell, Reuben Wood, Mary Wood, and Betsy Gibson. At the opening, the number of scholars was 30, which had increased by the close of the year following to 180, and twelvemonths later to 290. Both sexes were taught in the same room until April 27, 1851, when the new school adjoining was used for the boys, whilst the girls continued in the one previously occupied. The school was supported by private subscription until October, 1852, since which period annual collections for the purpose have been made in the church. The popularity and success of the school are chiefly to be ascribed to the constant and punctual attendance of the rector, coupled with his energy and aptitude for imparting instruction.

CLAYTON CHAPEL OF EASE AND CHURCH SCHOOL.

The nominal district of Clayton is co-extensive with the hamlet of that name, and contains an estimated population of 1,600 persons. On the 26th of March, 1854, the Rev. P. Thompson, B.A., opened a branch Sunday school under the superintendance of Mr. James Barrington, assisted by eight teachers, in a cottage house at West End, near Clayton Hall, when forty-two scholars were admitted.

In order to secure a more efficient parochial supervision, the Pastoral Aid Society made an annual grant of £100 towards supplying the stipends for a curate; and on June 12, 1845, the Rev. Joseph Renatus Walshaw, B.A., was licensed to the curacy of Droylsden; and he thenceforth resided in the district of Clayton, and assumed the superintendence of the Sabbath school. Four days afterwards, the foundation stone of a new day and Sunday school, a portion to be used for divine service, was laid by Mr. S. C. Trapp, agent to P. R. Hoare, Esq., at whose expense the edifice was erected. The cottage above named was licensed for divine service on the 1st of July, 1855, and there for twelve-months Mr. Walshaw continued to officiate. On his removal to Halifax, the congregation presented him with a parting token of esteem. Owing to circumstances, which it is unnecessary to explain, the curacy remained void until the 10th of the following March, when the Rev. Frederick Charles Woodhouse, M.A., of St. John's College, Cambridge, was nominated to fill the vacancy. In the meantime, Mr. Barrington was again appointed to the office of school superintendent.

The opening of the new school was delayed until March 9, 1857, when it was first brought into requisition as a day school, and, the licence being transferred, divine worship and Sabbath tuition quickly followed. The first baptism occurs on the 29th of the same month. The edifice, which is a neat brick structure in the form of the letter T, was erected at the expense of P. R. Hoare, Esq., whose plans include master's residence, church, and parsonage house, for

which contiguous sites are reserved. The interior is plain,
but agreeable; the ceilings are timbered and open to the
roofs.   The side walls of the chapel are adorned with
admonitory texts of Scripture, inscribed within ornamental
scrolls, and the eastern window, in imitation of stained glass,
is illuminated diaphonically, which well sustains the illusion.
Chapel accommodation is afforded for 100 adults and 100
children.

After the Rev. Mr. Woodhouse was appointed to the
rectory of St. Mary's, Hulme, Manchester, in November
last, he was followed at Clayton by the Rev. William
Walker Woollcombe, M.A., the present curate.

FAIRFIELD.

The United Brethren, usually called Moravians, had
founded a congregation at Dukinfield in 1755; but it was
deemed advisable to establish a settlement in the neighbourhood—in other words, a village, inhabited almost exclusively by members of their own community.   After
considerable difficulty and delay, they took possession, in
October, 1783, of an eligible piece of land of about sixty
acres, which they purchased on chief for 999 years from
Edward Greaves, Esq., of Culcheth Hall.

The erection of Fairfield was commenced on the 9th of
June, in the year following, with the laying of the foundation stone of the chapel, accompanied with suitable religious
solemnities.   So industriously was the work of building
prosecuted that the village was erected in little more than
a year, the chapel and contiguous square being first built,
and the other wings added shortly afterwards.

The chapel was solemnly opened for divine worship on
Sunday, July 17, 1785, with public and private services, a
sermon being preached by Brother Benjamin Latrobe. The
services were so numerously attended that many persons
could not gain admittance.   For above quarter of a century
this chapel remained the only place of worship in the
township.

Fairfield is situated on a gentle slope, has a southern
aspect, and fronts the Ashton Old-road, which lies at a field's

distance. The ground plot of the village is laid out with taste, and forms a large and commodious square. The front consists of a block of brick buildings, with the chapel in the centre. Rows of dwelling houses run on each side of the chapel. Another row in the rear completes the square. Broad paved streets, with flagged footpaths, pass between piles of buildings, which encompass three sides of the square. The whole, except on the north side, is encircled with orchards, pleasure grounds, and gardens.

The chapel is a plain brick edifice, surmounted with a cupola, terminating with a vane, and containing a public clock, and a bell for striking the hours, and calling the brethren to worship. The interior is commodious and agreeable, though characterised by simplicity of arrangement. The pulpit is fixed against the wall; and in front, slightly raised above the floor, stands the reading desk, used for the frequent devotional exercises of the community. Opposite to the pulpit, a gallery occupies the entire length of the chapel, in the centre of which stands an organ of excellent tone. Both the gallery and the body of the structure are filled with plain seats, arranged for the separation of the sexes.

By a statute of 1749, the Church of the United Brethren is recognised in this country as an "ancient Protestant Episcopal Church." In their public worship, the Moravians use a form of liturgy not unlike in its spirit that of the Church of England. This small body of Christians, considering its limited number of members, and its disclaiming proselytism abroad, is remarkable for its extraordinary activity and success in missionary enterprise.

Opposite the chapel, but with playgrounds and gardens intervening, is located the graveyard, appropriately ornamented with shrubs, evergreens, and a sun dial, inscribed "Lat. 53, 30. I Die to-day and Live to-morrow. 1790." In the graveyard the sexes are separated, even in death. Each grave is six feet deep, and none are ever reopened; but space is economised by plots being reserved for the separate interment of children and adults. A small square stone is placed at the head of each grave; and the only memento of the virtues or history of its occupant consists of a brief record of name, age, and time of departure.

Adjoining the chapel, on the one hand, is the residence of the minister, and, on the other, the seminary for young ladies. At the eastern extremity of the front is the Sisters' House, an establishment where a number of female members, employing themselves in needlework and embroidery, voluntarily reside in single blessedness, as did formerly the bachelor brethren, in the corresponding building in the west end.

The private houses were first inhabited principally by emigrants from the Moravian congregation at Dukinfield, which was not, however, altogether abandoned, but still exists in a flourishing state. In 1832, according to Holmes's "History of the United Brethren," there were 339 members in Fairfield; but at present the number may be somewhat less, as families belonging to other religious persuasions now reside in the settlement. The number of inhabitants is about 400; and everything about the village wears an air of comfort and peace. The streets are broad and spacious, sewered, and lighted with gas, and filtered water is supplied to the inhabitants.

FAIRFIELD SUNDAY SCHOOL.

This was the first Moravian Sunday School ever established, and the honour of its formation belongs to Mr. Henry Nalty and Mr. Frank Mallalieu, the former of whom lived to witness its jubilee. Schools for both sexes were opened on or about January 20, 1793, with some thirty or forty children.

The Boys' School was begun in a wing of the Brethren's House, in a room reached by an external flight of steps, and was only removed from thence on October 8, 1854, when the National School was opened.

The Girls' School was commenced at Lane Head, in the room subsequently occupied by the Wesleyans. The first teacher was Alice Hickson, who was afterwards despatched from Fairfield to the Cape of Good Hope; after labouring there faithfully for a great many years, she at last died in

Germany. The school was some time after removed to the premises previously used as a warehouse by Mr. Cresswell, and now occupied by Mr. Hines. Another removal took place to some rooms in the Sisters' House; and lastly, in 1817, the present school room was erected.

The first collection on behalf of these schools was made after a sermon preached by the Rev. John Swertner. Copies of the programme of hymns used on that and three succeeding anniversaries are now in the possession of Mr. Bowker, of Fairfield. The earliest programme issued consists of two small pages, containing the "Anthems and hymns to be sung at the chapel at Fairfield, near Manchester, on Sunday, November 3, 1793, in the afternoon at two o'clock, when a sermon will be preached for the benefit of the Sunday schools in Droylsdon township." The letterpress is surmounted with a wood cut, representing a trumpet and lyre reposing on an opened book, and the whole is enwreathed with a chaplet of flowers. First on the list appears the anthem, "Comfort ye my people"; then a hymn of six verses, the first four to be sung by the children, and the two last by all present; and finally the musical performances close with another anthem. The programme for the third year is comprised in four pages with the same heading as the first, except that the date is altered to August 9, 1795. Strangely enough, the same error in the orthography of the township is perpetuated. The only apparent novelty consists in the boys and girls taking separate lines in a hymn of twelve verses. The seventh anniversary was held October 27, 1799, and the ninth on June 14, 1801. For some time after their commencement, both writing and arithmetic were taught in the schools; but these were afterwards taught on the week nights instead. At the outset the boys were principally instructed by the boarding school teachers, for which purpose three teachers in turn attended for three Sundays in succession. Shortly afterwards a stipendiary teacher, Joseph Wood, was appointed, and with him were associated several voluntary assistants; and the whole arrangements were superintended by a staff of visitors, consisting of a number of householders, who, in rotation,

attended every Sabbath. In the morning, after the conclusion of public service in the chapel, the scholars were
conducted to the "children's meeting," when a short special
exhortation was delivered, and in the afternoon it was
customary to take them to the ordinary public service.

WESLEYAN METHODISM.

Only meagre recollections and notices, unfortunately, have
survived respecting the first introduction of Methodism into
the locality, and of its progress during the incursionary
period, when local preachers from Manchester visited the
neighbouring villages and supplemented the efforts of zealous
converts, who, as in Droylsden, preached the gospel in one
another's houses.

The first Methodist sermon recorded to have been delivered in the township was preached, it is said, by John
Ashton, from an oak tree which stood near the entrance to
the present Recreation Grounds. Shortly afterwards, meetings for prayer and preaching were established in a cottage,
now divided into two, adjoining the King's Head. The
earliest definite record of Methodism in Droylsden occurs in
connection with this domicile. The Grimshaws, in their
obituary register, have inserted the names of various
preachers at Lane Head, together with the texts and dates
of their sermons. Thus, in 1779, on the 11th of July, and
the four following Sabbaths, the officiators were Mr. Gibson
(2 Cor. v. 20), Richard Emon, John Kenerly, William
Clayton, and John Boon. After a blank interval, it is noticed
that James Kenyon preached on September 19, in the same
year, Mr. Benson on the 19th of the following April, and,
lastly, Mr. Vaulton on April 17, 1781, after which the
authority is silent. It is recollected that a few years subsequently, the Methodists of Droylsden and Openshaw met
for worship on some occasions at Henry Hallam's, in Little
Droylsden, and on others at Robert Turner's, in Back Openshaw. In the barn adjoining, annual sermons were delivered and love feasts held. A few years afterwards, as
is remembered, there was preaching on Sunday afternoons at Thomas Selby's, in Little Droylsden, and in the

G

evening at Joseph Lowe's, near Lane End, in Droylsden.
The first Wesleyan Society in the township was established
in or about 1806; and from that time permanent services
were commenced at Lane End in an upper room of a three
storeyed building, which, a few years ago, was replaced by
the shop now held by Mrs. Parker. The basement storey
was a cellar, and an external flight of nine or ten steps
afforded access to the intermediate floor, occupied by Thomas
Mather, a cobbler. From this floor ingress was obtained to
the meeting room above.

For many years no special effort was made for the young;
but, at the conclusion of a class meeting, one Monday evening, in January, 1819, a few young men and women, after
due consideration, resolved to commence a Sabbath school.
On the following Sunday, at its opening, the teachers outnumbered the scholars. The teachers were John Grimshaw,
John Thornley, Jeremiah Etchells, John Etchells, Benjamin
Kenyon, Esther Schofield, Ann Lowe, and Betty, Esther,
and Alice Hill, who, as well as the children, brought, to
begin with, what spare Bibles and spelling books they could
procure.

The first collection was made in July, 1819, at the close
of a sermon preached from Isaiah liv. 13, by Mr. William
Blackburn, in a barn which stood nearly opposite. In this
barn the several anniversaries were held till the opening of
the new chapel. The second yearly sermon was preached
by Mr. John Crawshaw, and the third by Mr. W. Pollard,
in June, 1821, when upwards of 200 children were receiving
gratuitous instruction.

Although the second storey had been brought into use,
yet, owing to the influx of scholars, the premises became
inconveniently small. An eligible plot of land having been
procured from Thomas Greene, Esq., on Friday, August 5,
1825, the foundation stone of a new chapel was laid by the
Rev. P. C. Turner, who delivered an appropriate address.
The same minister also preached on the wakes Tuesday,
from Matthew vii. 24, in the shell of the building, then
about shoulder height. The opening took place on or
about the third Sabbath in April, 1826, with three sermons

preached by the Revs. Robert Newton (Mark xvi. 5), John
Waterhouse (Luke x. 41-2), and Jabez Bunting (1 Tim. iv. 8).

The chapel, which is palisaded from Market-street, is a
plain but compact brick erection, and measures, internally,
thirty-seven feet square. A stone panel, inscribed "Wesleyan Chapel, 1825," is inserted in. the entrance gable,
which is pierced by two lower and three upper windows.
There are, also, three windows on each side of the building.
Thus the interior is well lighted, and is airy and neatly
furnished. Including a small eastern gallery, there are 350
sittings, of which 100 are free. The cost of erection and
improvement, up to January, 1829, was £603, for £450 of
which the trustees are still responsible ; and, in addition,
the current debt amounts to above £40. The site contains
553 square yards, leased on an annual chief of £2 6s. 3d. ;
and the acting trustee is Mr. C. Beswick, of Manchester.
The trust deed, which is enrolled in Chancery, is similar in
purport to those by which Wesleyan chapels are generally
held.

A small Sunday school, capable of accommodating eighty
children, and restricted to the junior classes, was built in
1828 in the rear of the chapel, in which edifice the senior
scholars continued to be taught. At length, in order to
remedy the inconvenience, the present school of two storeys,
with four class rooms, was erected on the old site, at a cost
of £220, and opened for use on the 6th of October, 1850. A
bazaar in aid of the building fund was held in the premises
on the fifth and several succeeding days of the following
month, which, supplementing a public subscription, realised
a sufficient amount to defray the expense of erection.

PRIMITIVE METHODISM.

Several Primitive Methodists from Stockport, including
Mr. William Stafford, of Woodley, visited Droylsden as
missionaries about August, 1836. One Sunday evening,
after preaching in a house near the Copperas Works, Mr.
Stafford intimated that it was intended to form a society,
when five persons accepted the invitation, and enrolled
their names on the class paper. The number increasing

shortly afterwards, they engaged the room at Lane End, sometime held by the Wesleyans, and there commenced assembling for worship, and opened a Sabbath school as well.

Being obliged, after a brief period, to vacate the premises, the school was relinquished, but the society continued to meet, first at William Moor's, then at Peter Turner's, and afterwards evening service was begun in the Temperance Room, which was sublet to them by the Independents, who used it themselves in the morning and afternoon.

After a time, subscriptions were obtained towards erecting a new chapel; and having secured a site at Lane Head, a small but neat structure of brick was erected at an expense of £150, of which £80 still remains as a debt. A stone label in front is inscribed, "Primitive Methodist Chapel, erected 1845." The opening took place February 23, 1845, and the services extended over the succeeding Sunday, and concluded on the following (Monday) evening. In 1856, the entrance door was removed into Chapel-street, the edifice enlarged to 10 yards by 7, and the seat accommodation increased from 150 to 200 persons, at an expense of £50, borne by subscription. Since the opening, it has been used for the purpose of a Sabbath school.

PROMISCUOUS.

Besides those religious bodies which gained a footing in the village, incursionary efforts were made by zealous disciples of other sects.

About 1834, a Mr. Collins, who taught a small day school in the premises subsequently occupied as the temperance room, used the same place on Sundays for preaching. The Warrenites afterwards held the room for a time; and they were followed by the admirers of the Rev. Joseph R. Stevens. But as all these efforts were of a temporary character, no appreciable result followed.

INDEPENDENCY.

The principles of Congregationalism, or Independency, were preached early in the seventeenth century at Gorton Chapel, when and where, probably, they were imbibed by the Jollies, the first known family in Droylsden belonging to that persuasion. Later on, Oliver Heywood, the celebrated Nonconformist minister, as recorded in his diary, preached on January 6, 1667, at night (for secresy), at the house of James Hulton, of Droisden, an old Commonwealth officer.

Modern Independency was introduced into Droylsden soon after the starting of Fairfield Mills. Apparently, in December, 1837, Messrs. Lee Meaden, John Hartley, and George Shaw commenced a Sabbath school in the premises afterwards known as the Temperance Room, and on the first Sunday had about four teachers and twenty scholars. In the course of a few months, public service and preaching were also begun in the same place.

Mr. W. M. Christy, having erected a new school room in Queen-street early in 1838, granted its use to the conductors of the above school, for the purpose of instructing " children of all denominations," free from sectarianism, and without public preaching. However, after a year or two had elapsed, on the understanding that the principle on which the school was conducted would not be interfered with, permission was obtained from Mr. Christy to use the room for preaching on Sunday evenings. This was inaugurated by the Rev. Jonathan Sutcliffe, F.S.A., of Ashton-under-Lyne, who, some years before, had preached occasionally in a dwelling house at Lum, on the confines of Droylsden. From that period, although the school remained unsectarian, yet the public worship was strictly congregational, all the officiating ministers belonging to that persuasion. In the week following the first Sabbath in February, 1845, when the scholars had increased to between one and two hundred, the managers of the building transferred the use of the room to the recently appointed incumbent of Droylsden.

After an intermission of one or two Sundays, a few of the

old teachers, having rented the Temperance Room, recom-
menced both the Sabbath school and evening service, though
the former was discontinued shortly afterwards.

Messrs. Charles Barker, Lee Meaden,'and a few associates,
in the autumn of 1846, resolved on again reopening the
Sunday school, and the former person consented to become
superintendent.

At first, the scholars were few in number, but gradually
increased, until the room became inconveniently small. The
service was afterwards changed from evening to morning
and afternoon. Under the impression that the building was
about to be taken down, subscriptions were begun for the
purpose of erecting a new school room or chapel. To promote this object a circular was issued, without date, but
apparently near the close of 1846, and signed by Mr. Charles
Barker, superintendent, and Messrs. Benjamin Halcrow,
Lee Meaden, Edward Warren, Andrew Robertson, and John
Ashburn, committee men.

A site was obtained in King-street, then an open field,
and on a portion of it they erected a rectangular edifice,
capable of seating nearly 200 persons. The memorial stone
in front is labelled, " Droylsden Independent Sunday School,
1847." The interior is lighted by two pointed windows in
front, and four square headed ones on each side. The
internal porch, pulpit, forms with backs, stove, and gas
apparatus, are neat, but of plain design. There is a class
room or vestry attached, and the premises are vested in
trustees, and registered according to law.

The school room was opened for divine worship on Feb.
20, 1848, the Rev. Dr. Massie, of Salford, preaching in the
afternoon and the Rev. J. Sutcliffe in the evening, and the
Rev. W. W. Essex, of Fairfield, on the following (Monday)
evening. A small debt was left on the building, but happily
extinguished a few years afterwards.

For a time the students of the Lancashire Independent College and others officiated at the chapel; but at length a grant
was obtained from the Congregational Union, and promises of
other assistance were received, for the purpose of maintaining
a stated minister. Choice fell upon the Rev. David Wilson,

who, on the 3rd of October, 1852, commenced his pastoral duties in Droylsden. At the end of twelve months, he removed to Ryton, near Newcastle-upon-Tyne. His successor was the Rev. Thomas Sturges, who preached his first sermon in Droylsden on the 16th of October, 1853, and his last on the 11th of January, 1857, when he removed to Upper Mill, in Saddleworth, where he is still located. The Rev. Charles Bingley, of Tockholes, near Blackburn, commenced preaching at Droylsden August 9, 1857, and is the present respected minister of the congregation. The church here assembling was affiliated to that at Albion-street Chapel, Ashton-under-Lyne, until October 25, 1857, when it was rendered independent.

Having long felt the inconvenience of meeting for worship in a room devoted to Sabbath school purposes, strenuous efforts were made to realise funds for the erection of a new chapel. A bazaar, for the sale of fancy articles, was held in a large marquee, near Seventhorns' Wells, on the seventh and three following days of July, 1858; and three services were held and collections made in the same place, on the Sabbath ensuing.

A site was obtained opposite Droylsden Mills, with a frontage to Market-street. The foundation stone was laid on the 25th of April, 1859, by Abel Buckley, Esq., of Alderdale Lodge, Droylsden, and the event was commemorated with a tea meeting in the evening.

The chapel will be in the decorated Gothic style of architecture, the exterior walls being faced with red and white bricks, relieved with dressings of York stone. The front to Market-street will be fifty-three feet wide, and, including the porches, divided into five compartments, the centre one containing a large four light window, with flamboyant tracery in the head.

The school rooms are placed underneath the chapel; but the foundation being only seven feet below, and the chapel floor six feet above, the level of Market-street, the school rooms will have many of the advantages in light and ventilation of an upper room. The main school room is thirty-five feet square, with nine commodious class rooms opening out of it, including an infant class room twenty-two feet by thirteen feet. Most of the class room doors are arranged to fold, so that all can be thrown open for occasional large public meetings.

The chapel consists of the main room, which will be built of sufficient loftiness to permit of the introduction of future galleries. The entrances to the chapel will be from the before mentioned porches, which will be ample and well provided with swing doors, with the upper panels glazed with plate glass. At the back of the chapel is a projection containing the vestry, back staircase, &c. The tower will be surmounted with a graceful spire, and will contain the staircase to future galleries. The whole is intended to be surrounded by fence walls, with ornamental iron gates and rails to the Market-street front. There will be accommodation for 391 adults on the ground floor, and the galleries which may be inserted at any future time will be constructed to contain 238 persons, making a total of 629 adults.

The architect is Mr. R. Moffat Smith, of Manchester, and the builders, Messrs. Bates, Baguley, and Co., of Droylsden. The cost of the whole is estimated not to exceed £1,900, and, including the proceeds of the late bazaar, the sale of the school room, the subscriptions, promises, &c., it is hoped to open the chapel free from debt.

EDGE-LANE AND EAST END CHAPEL AND SUNDAY SCHOOL.

In the early part of 1850, Mr. Jabez Ashworth took a house, or shop, at East End, at a shilling a week rent, and opened it as a Sabbath school. Mr. Ashworth, on the first Sunday, was the only teacher, and about half a dozen little children came for instruction; but gradually additional teachers and scholars both fell in. After some three years occupation, the room at East End was exchanged for larger premises in Edge-lane, rented from Mr. Harrop at £4 per annum. These were formerly an outhouse and granary, and consist of two storeys, used for school purposes, and the lower one used for evening service, being furnished with seats, pulpit, and harmonium. In the earlier stages of the school, a local preacher, connected with the Wesleyan Association, came occasionally to officiate. Afterwards, it had some association with the Moravians, but is not now considered as attached to any denomination.

Mr. Ashworth's connection terminated with his removal to Gorton Brook, and the teachers and scholars, on Christmas Day, 1857, presented him with a parting token of esteem. Mr. Foulds Sutcliffe was his successor in the office of superintendent.

NEW CONNECTION METHODISTS.

This body of Christians for some years has possessed a small chapel at Moor-lane, in Openshaw, which, being close to the boundaries of Droylsden, has caused it to be resorted to by some of the villagers.

A deputation from a similar society at Hooley Hill, having taken a shop in Hallas's-buildings, Manchester-road, commenced Divine service on the 16th May, 1858, in one of the rooms capable of accommodating some sixty persons, the opening sermons being preached by the Rev. Stanley Jackson, of Ashton-under-Lyne. Afterwards, on the 11th of July, under the superintendence of Mr. James Mallalieu, of Droylsden, a Sabbath school was begun, with only three scholars. The scholars, on the Sabbath succeeding, increased to thirty.

LATTER-DAY SAINTS.

The Mormons, some years ago, obtained a slight footing in the township, and opened a meeting room in Edward-street ; but public indignation being aroused by their breaking the ice on the canal to immerse a convert, they found it advisable to desist advocating their tenets. In April, 1852, another attempt was made to establish Mormonism, in Edge-lane, but was relinquished. And, finally, in October, 1857, they assailed the township at Clayton, but met with a vigorous repulse.

ROMAN CATHOLICISM.

Droylsden contains a considerable number of Roman Catholics, almost without exception natives of the Sister Isle. Their place of worship, St. Ann's Chapel, is locally situated within Openshaw, but contiguous to Droylsden, and frequently takes its designation therefrom. The building was originally erected as a warehouse, and consists of three storeys, the lower one being used as the boys' Sunday school, the upper one for the girls, and the intermediate storey, which is fitted up for worship, was, on the 28th October, 1849, opened as a temporary chapel. Funds are now being collected to erect a new edifice.

RELIGIOUS AND EDUCATIONAL STATISTICS.

In 1845, the Rev. P. Thompson, B.A., made a house to house visitation of 450 families in the village, with the following results. The number of persons was 2,493, including 1,352 children, chiefly under sixteen years of age. In some houses he found two or three families, and in several from two to four lodgers. Their religious views were thus analysed: Families professing to belong to the Wesleyan Methodists, 38; Church of England, 30; Primitive Methodists, 7; Moravians, 6; Independents, 5; Roman Catholics, 3; Baptists, 2; New Connection Methodists, 2; Quakers, 1; Socinians, 1; making no religious profession and attending no religious ordinance, 355; total, 450. "What a startling fact!" says the inquirer. "Within the parish of Manchester, and but four miles from the centre of the town, which for energy, wealth, and institutions is the admiration of the civilised world, above 350 families out of 450, live without God in the world. I doubt much if the statistics of the chief town of Tahiti would furnish so melancholy a result." Of the 1,352 children above mentioned, the number attending day schools was: British School, 70; infant department, 60; Old School and a small private one, 37; total, 167. Attending Sunday schools: Wesleyan Methodist, 260; Church of England, 180; Moravian, 68; New

Connection (school not in township), 65 ; Primitive Methodist, 50 ; Roman Catholic (school not in township), 10 ; making a total of 633.

Secular Education.—Returns were solicited from the several schools in the township, and the following exhibits the numbers under tuition in April last. The only objection to furnish particulars arose from Fairfield day and boarding schools, which are almost restricted to non-residents, and in numbers, so far as Droylsden is concerned, do not more than compensate for the Roman Catholic children who are sent to the school in Openshaw :—

School.	On Register.			In Attendance.		
	M.	F.	Total	M.	F.	Total
Queen-st., British (Juvenile)	270	130	400	190	90	280
,, ,, (Infant)...	110	90	200	90	70	160
Fairfield, Day School.........	110	60	170	100	48	148
Clayton, Church	69	54	123	66	44	110
Clayton Vale, National	120	24	144	70	20	90
Total.....................	679	358	1037	516	272	788

There are likewise normal or dame schools kept in Droylsden village, at Fairfield, East End, and Edge-lane, possessing an aggregate of eighty pupils. If the children of all ages and both sexes in the township be estimated at 4,000, the number fit to attend school may be computed at 1,400, or all those between three and nine years of age, which are the respective limits at which children are admitted into the infant schools and the factories.

The above statistics include seventy "short timers" from the mills attending Queen-street School, and the like number from the printworks frequenting that at Clayton Vale. Hence, it appears that nearly 900 are receiving education under the voluntary system, and 140 under the Printworks and Factory Acts, leaving nearly 500, and three fourths of them females, as attending no school at all.

Religious Education.—The following authentic table is compiled (with the exception of Fairfield Sunday school, which has been obtained from private sources) from the average of returns made on the two first Sabbath afternoons in April last :—

	On Register.					In Attendance.				
	Teachers		Scholars.			Teachers.		Scholars.		
	M.	F.	M.	F.	Total	M.	F.	M.	F.	Total
Church	27	24	304	318	622	13	12	222½	215½	438
,, (Clayton)	15	15	112	117	229	12	8	85½	89½	175
Wesleyan	24	17	210	233	443	19½	16½	165	199½	364½
Independent...	9	16	132	155	287	8	8	89½	89	178½
Prim. Meth. ...	10	9	42	50	92	5½	4½	33½	37½	71
New Con.	8	4	32	34	66	6½	3½	28	30½	58½
Edge-lane	7	4	44	87	131	5½	4	28½	55	83½
Moravian	9	15	72	90	162	6	6	50	73	123
Total	109	104	948	1084	2032	76	62½	702½	789½	1492

Hence, it appears that more than one fourth of the population are receiving religious instruction on the Sabbath ; and, assuming 2,500 to be of an age fit to attend, it follows that in the entire township there are only 467 children who never resort to any Sunday school.

The teachers connected with the Independent, Wesleyan, and Primitive Methodist schools on the 10th of May, 1855, founded a Sunday School Teachers' Association, which at present remains in abeyance.

LITERATURE, LECTURES, ELOCUTION, ETC.

Hitherto few persons, whether natives or residents, have by their labours in the cause of literature, science, or art, achieved even local fame.

Elias Hall, of Droylsden, left a curious MS. history of the Oldham choir, in or about 1695, and also published something on the same subject. Amongst modern authors and *literateurs*, Messrs. James Burgess, George Wadlow, and Edward and William Rayner have written various fugitive and detached poetical effusions, and Mr. Samuel Lees divers moral and political sketches, reviews, &c.

Lecturing in the present day forms an important element in the diffusion of knowledge. Mr. J. W. Slater has delivered interesting lectures on chemistry, natural history,

&c.; Rev. P. Thompson on the history of Turkey, Rev. T. Sturges on the Crimean war, Messrs. J. Burgess and E. Rayner on poetry and elocution, Messrs. S. Dawson and R. Wood on physical geography, Messrs. W. Chorlton and J. J. Hulme on Sunday school economy, and Mr. D. Bolton on the steam engine and electricity. The most singular subject was chosen by a non-resident lady, who, in November, 1852, lectured at a public house on the "Bloomer Costume."

Apart from lecturing and preaching, up to the present the science of oratory has been little studied in the locality. With the exception of a few tea meeting speakers, and trade and political declaimers, teetotalism has almost stood alone in producing public speakers, generally notable more for energetic than classical language, and including Messrs. J. Dennis, J. Deaken, E. L. Jenkins, A. Barlow, P. Etchells, J. Fitton, J. Holgate, and J. Withington. There are numerous reciters; and a few public readers sprang up in the winter of 1857-8 on the adoption of free public readings, held on Friday evenings, in the Educational Institution.

There are several circulating libraries in the township, which contain an aggregate of 3,950 volumes, but have only 350 readers. These are the library of the Educational Institution, originated by the Mechanics' Institution and Young Men's Association in 1848; Droylsden Mills, 1841; Angola Mill, 1856; Wesleyan Sunday School, 1828; Church, 1846; Independent, 1851; Primitive, 1852; Edgelane, 1853; Clayton, February 7, 1859; and the Queenstreet British School, 1850. There are three or four newsvendors and stationers, a depot of the Christian Knowledge Society, and religious tracts are distributed by the Independents and Moravians.

A spirited effort was made in May, 1854, to supply the locality with a literary and advertising medium, under the title of *The Droylsden Literary and Advertising Journal*, a miscellany of four pages, which was sold for one halfpenny. After issuing nine monthly numbers and obtaining a circulation of 1,100 copies, the undertaking was reluctantly abandoned from a lack of local advertising patronage.

INNS AND PUBLIC HOUSES.

At a period not very remote, Droylsden, owing to its location "on the road to nowhere," or rather from its not being situated on any public thoroughfare connecting adjacent towns, could not boast of a single public house. In the Commonwealth era, the tipplers apparently resorted to Manchester, as Justice Hibbert, of Droylsden, was drowned whilst inebriated, in November, 1657, on returning from that town.   Probably, the blacksmith's shop supplied the place of the public house as a rendezvous for gossips, Droylsden, apparently, having its smithy in the sixteenth century, and its smith certainly in 1689 in the person of Thomas Heape.

The Red Lion, in Little Droylsden, was an early wayside hostelry, and is said to have been the first in the township. Its owner and occupant, John Thelwell, alias " Old Maccaroni," on the diversion of the road, erected the new Red Lion, now the Halfway House, Openshaw, got the licence transferred, and died there in July, 1789.

A duplicate Red Lion, the first dwelling on the north side of Far-lane, near the King's Head, was once kept by James Hill, who, inflamed with jealousy, suddenly disappeared, and, about a fortnight afterwards, was found hung or strangled in a tree in Newton Wood, near Hyde.   A coroner's inquest pronounced it an act of suicide, and, in accordance with the verdict, the corpse was interred on the 21st of May, 1774, at three lane ends, near the brook, close by the present Commercial Inn, Newton Moor.   Much sympathy was exhibited towards Hill in Droylsden, and a band of resolute fellows about three o'clock on the morning of the 5th of June disinterred his remains, and reburied them in Ashton churchyard. A woman who casually met them spread the information, and they were glad to convey back the body on the 16th of the same month, when the final interment took place at Newton Moor. A number of Droylsdenians joined to defray the expense of a grave stone, on which the following epitaph, written by Joseph Willan, of Openshaw, was neatly engraved :—

" Here was Deposited the Body of the unfortunate

James Hill,

Late of Droylsden, who ended his Life May 6th, 1774,
In the forty-second year of his age.

Unhappy Hill, with anxious Cares oppress'd,
Rashly presumed to find in Death his Rest.
With this vague Hope in Lonesome Wood did he
Strangle himself, as Jury did agree ;
For which a Christian burial he's denied,
And is consign'd to Lie at this wayside.

READER !
REFLECT WHAT MAY BE THE CONSEQUENCES OF A CRIME WHICH
EXCLUDES THE POSSIBILITY OF REPENTANCE."

The Red Lion was afterwards kept by " Old" John Hulme, who, in May, 1782, established a club for women's stays, then a rare article of dress. The White Hart has been used as an ale house since November, 1781. An early " hush shop" in Green-lane bore the unique sign of the " Jack Ass Head," which was literally the skull of a donkey. The township, in 1834, contained six public houses, and, eighteen years later, when the shops of every description only numbered fifty-two, there were thirty-two inns and beer houses, being on an average one for every 203 inhabitants, *inclusive of children !*

TEETOTALISM.

Temperance, total abstinence, or teetotal societies—the last designation, from a Lancashire word, signifying entire abstinence from intoxicating beverages, being the popular one—hold a distinguished place amongst moral and benevolent associations.

Previous to 1836, there was a moderation movement at work in Droylsden ; but what progress it made or what benefit it conferred upon the inhabitants does not appear. In March of that year, after six weeks' canvass, Mr. Joseph Ellor had the honour of founding the first teetotal society in the township. A committee of seven persons was appointed.

The society continued to assemble for four years in the
Wesleyan Chapel, when the further loan of the place was
declined. The society was then removed to the premises
opposite Durham-street end, now known as the Old Teetotal
Room, and there held stated public meetings, committee
meetings, &c., until its dissolution. After several subsequent ineffectual attempts, a juvenile society was established
in January, 1847. At one time, it had no less than seventy-
five members, with an attendance of sixty at a night school,
kept in a cottage in Edward-street, where spelling, reading,
writing, and arithmetic were gratuitously taught to the
members. Unfortunately, it became defunct in April, 1849.

The adult society attained its zenith of prosperity in
1849, during which year no less than 267 persons signed
the teetotal pledge. In the following year, tracts on total
abstinence were circulated in the village at the rate of four
hundred per week, and a first rate procession was got up
on the Monday of the wakes week. The members wore
white rosettes, and the juveniles were distinguished by a
strip of blue. A red herring, borne on a pole, was inscribed
" A Drunkard's Bullock," and an empty barrel was labelled
" To Let." A wooden legged personator of an inebriate,
riding on an ass, was abused in Fairfield by a real tippler,
as " drunk as a lord," and evidently averse to shams.

But the cause declined; and, although a tolerable procession was mustered in May, 1850, the society ceased to
exist a few months afterwards.

Fairfield, for about sixty-three years, possessed a noted
inn ; but the synod which met in Germany, in October,
1848, recommending the closing of all places for the manufacture and sale of intoxicating drinks within its jurisdiction, the Fairfield establishment has since been used as a
board and lodging house.

A Band of Hope was instituted in connection with the
Wesleyan Sabbath School, on the 26th of August, 1852,
when twenty of the teachers took the pledge. Shortly
afterwards, there were thirty-two of the teachers and sixty-
one of the scholars members of the society. The society,
in March, 1853, merged into the Droylsden Temperance

League, then originated under the presidency of the Rev. David Wilson, for the purpose of furthering the temperance cause in the Sabbath schools and among the different Christrian congregations. When the United Kingdom Alliance was formed, in October, 1853, the committee of the Droylsden League agreed to co-operate with that movement, and so continued until October, 1856, when they discontinued operations, and on the 16th of April following finally dissolved the association.

A petition for closing public houses on the Sabbath was despatched from Droylsden in May, 1854, with 535 signatures attached. At present there is a Band of Hope in connection with the Independent Sabbath School; and also, under the auspices of a few teetotalers, lectures are occasionally delivered in the Wesleyan School Room.

PROVIDENT INSTITUTIONS.

The industrial classes are able to alleviate much suffering and distress by joining various secret orders, and other less formal friendly societies and clubs, instituted, in most cases, as well for relief of members when sick as for interment when dead.

The most ancient association in the village is the Old Men's Club, a branch of a sick society begun in Openshaw so far back as 1777, with eighty-one members. A division of members and funds subsequently took place. One section removed to Gorton, where it still exists; and the other to Fairfield New Inn; thence to the Bull's Head, Audenshaw; and finally settled down at the White Hart, Droylsden. A sick club, commenced in 1843, in connection with Fairfield Mills, is now extinct.

There are numerous lodges of the Independent Order of Odd Fellows (M.U.), Union Odd Fellows, Ancient Foresters, United Free Gardeners, Female Gardeners, Shepherds, and Druids. The Droylsden Charitable Burial Society, held at the King's Head, was established in 1841, and numbers now more than 3,000 members. There are burial clubs also connected with the Wesleyan and Church Sunday Schools; and in the village is a self-supporting Board of Health.

In addition to inviting relatives and friends from a distance, at funerals it was once customary to "lathe owth' foak ut liv't op th' loane." By that means a large concourse was collected, and, probably on the plea that "sorrow will have drink," they were copiously regaled with malt liquor. The average cost of several adult interments, as returned to a burial society eighty years ago, was £1 13s. 9½d., disposed of in the following manner :— Washing corpse, 1s.; coffin, 11s.; dues, 2s. 2d.; bread, 5s. 3d.; ale, 11s. 9d.; rum, 1s.; sugar, 1s.; nutmeg, 2d.; tobacco, 3½d.; and rosemary, 2d. About a dozen years afterwards, at another interment, the expense of which was defrayed by the township, the coffin, dues, suit, asking to the funeral, bread and cheese, only amounted to £1 1s. 0½d; whilst nearly as much, £1 0s. 4d., was lavished in rum, ale, sugar, and tobacco.

Many of the operatives support strikes, trade unions, and other societies, for the benefit or upholding of their respective branches of employment. A co-operative store, for the sale of groceries and provisions unadulterated and at a cheap scale of prices was wound up, after an existence of several years. A branch of the Manchester and Salford Savings Bank, in May, 1852, was begun at Openshaw, just without the boundaries of Droylsden, which furnishes a number of depositors and several inspectors of accounts. A penny preliminary savings bank was established, October, 1854, in connection with Fairfield National School, and has now seventy-four male and forty-six female depositors.

Clothing clubs, for the benefit of the scholars, are attached to the Church and Wesleyan Sabbath Schools. The Fairfield and Droylsden Bible Society was formed more than a quarter of a century ago; and auxiliary missionary and other similar societies are associated with most of the Sunday schools and places of worship.

Amongst the semi-provident societies existing are money clubs, furniture clubs, drapers' clothing clubs, and the like. A singular club, for procuring women's stays, was established so long ago as May, 1782, at the house of John Hulme. Although there are no building societies, yet a

singular and somewhat notorious scheme, called the Droylsden Property Division Lottery, was vigorously progressing
in May, 1859, when the Attorney-General took the matter
in hand, and caused it to be relinquished.

Questionable benefits have been derived also from *im*-
provident institutions, such as a loan society, raffles, trust
shops, travelling Scotchmen, and a couple of pawnshops.

LOCAL WORTHIES, CELEBRITIES, ETC.

In this niche, up to the present time, a few brief bio-
graphies may suffice,—not so, it is hoped, in the " good
time coming."

Humphrey Chetham, whose name stands out in fore-
most relief, is briefly noticed in a previous chapter.

Charles Hindley, Esq., was born at Fairfield, June 25,
1796, and died at Dartmouth House, Westminster, December 1, 1857, after representing Ashton-under-Lyne in
Parliament for more than twenty-three years. He was the
third son of Ignatius and Mary Hindley, and received the
rudiments of his education at the Moravian Academy, at
Fairfield, and afterwards at a similar establishment at Fulneck, near Leeds, and finally completed his studies with
the Rev. C. A. Pohlman, of Haverfordwest, South Wales.
After occupying, for several years, the position of classical
and mathematical tutor at the Moravian establishment,
Gracehill, Ireland, in February, 1819, on the death of his
brother, he undertook the management of a cotton mill, in
Dukinfield, in which he had previously been a sleeping
partner. Mr. Hindley was a steady friend and promoter of
the Short Time Bill, the Peace Society, mechanics' institutions, Sunday schools, and other benevolent institutions.

John Frederic Foster, Esq., was born at Wyke, near
Halifax, in 1795. His early education was partly acquired
at Fairfield, under the Rev. John Rogers. Subsequently he
was placed in the Moravian Academy at Fulneck, and afterwards completed his scholastic studies at Cambridge. Mr.
Foster was called to the bar in June, 1821, and subsequently
commenced practice as a barrister in Manchester, and for
some years resided in Fairfield. At that time, Mr. Foster

took an active interest in the parochial affairs of Droylsden, and, in December, 1825, was nominated a trustee of the Public Day School, an office which he retained till death. In August, 1825, Mr. Foster was appointed stipendiary magistrate for Manchester and Salford, and, in April, 1838, to the chairmanship of the quarter sessions for the hundred of Salford, in both of which spheres, successively, his conduct was exemplary, until suddenly cut off by death, on the 9th April, 1858, at his residence at Alderley, Cheshire.

The Rev. Benjamin La Trobe, an eminent Moravian minister, and a most excellent religious writer, esteemed by all evangelical persuasions, took a warm interest in Fairfield. The settlement was founded under his direction, and with his active co-operation, as provincial or superintendent of the congregations of the United Brethren in England. From Fulneck he was called to London, where he died, 29th November, 1786, aged fifty-eight years. An engraved portrait and brief memoir are inserted in Aikin's "Manchester and Forty Miles Round."

The Rev. Christian Ignatius La Trobe, son of the above, held the offices of secretary to the church and to the missions of the brethren. In musical attainments, he was second to none of his age in Great Britain, and, though an amateur, may be said to have done more than any other man to promote the cause of sacred music in this country. His own compositions, many of which were published, are of no ordinary excellence. After a residence of several years, he died at Fairfield, 6th May, 1836, aged seventy-eight, and was buried in the graveyard adjoining. He left four sons. Peter, the eldest, for three years had the superintendence of the Single Brethren's House in Fairfield. He was afterwards assistant to his father, and then succeeded him in his offices. John Antes is canon of Carlisle, and incumbent of St. Thomas's, Kendal. He is the author of several excellent works, including two volumes of poems, chiefly on sacred subjects. Charles Joseph was educated at Fulneck, and became a teacher in Fairfield School. Subsequently, he travelled much on foot, and became known to the reading public by his "Alpenstock Pedestrian and Rambler in North

America and Mexico." When Government made a grant for educational purposes, on the emancipation of slaves in the West Indies, he was nominated a commissioner, and afterwards was appointed superintendent and then lieutenant-governor of the colony of Victoria. Last year, for energetic and meritorious conduct in that capacity, he was created a Companion of the Bath. Frederick Benjamin, the fourth son, was brought up to medicine, and practised in the West Indies until 1841, when he died in Jamaica.

The Rev. William Wisdom Essex, bishop of the Church of the United Brethren, was born January 6, 1795, in the town of Devizes. It appears from an excellent biographical sketch (p. 33) that, in 1820, he became labourer of the Single Brethren at Fairfield, where, two years afterwards, he was ordained deacon by the late Bishop Moore, and in 1823 was called to be minister and director of the boys' and girls' schools at Gracehill. In 1842, Mr. Essex accepted the office of congregational helper and director of the girls' boarding school at Fairfield, which position he retained seven years. After various locations, his death took place May 31, 1850.

The Rev. John Rogers succeeded Mr. Essex at Fairfield. He was subsequently advanced to the episcopate of the Brethren, preached his farewell address at Fairfield, September 19, 1858, retired from the ministry, and settled at Bristol.

James Bowker was born at Fairfield, June 30, 1787, and died on the estate October 14, 1854, after residing there the greater portion of his life. He was partly of German extraction, his mother, Benigna Ockershausen, being the daughter of a Lutheran minister. Mr. Bowker was long employed in hand loom weaving, but during his latter years followed chiefly twisting-in at Edge-lane Mill. He possessed a sound judgment and powerful memory, and as a vocalist had paid professional visits to York and other places. He wrote an account of the early state of the cotton trade in the township, which appeared in the *Droylsden Literary and Advertising Journal;* and, after considerable addition and emendation, has been made use of in these pages.

Richard Oastler, Esq., the able advocate of "short time," resided for awhile in seclusion in Fairfield.

LOCAL BENEFACTORS.

Not a single charitable bequest is to be found in exclusive connection with Droylsden, and, even in joint participation with other places, Humphrey Chetham's benefactions have hitherto stood alone, the admiration of all. By his last will, dated at Clayton, December 16, 1651, Chetham bequeathed £7,000, to be expended in purchasing estates of the clear annual value of £420, to be employed in the founding and endowing of a hospital for maintaining, clothing, educating, bringing up, and apprenticing poor boys. Droylsden originally furnished three recipients, which, about 1700, were increased to four, eighty years later to six, and some time ago the number was further augmented to eight. After the founder's death, two long centuries were suffered to elapse without any monumental inscription being placed over his remains, when a gentleman, once, as a lad, an inmate of the hospital, who had been successful in business, erected a chaste stone statue to his memory in the Cathedral. The only memento of this truly local worthy to be found in Droylsden is in the sign of a roadside public house at Clayton.

The Byrons had previously been benefactors to Manchester Parish Church, and doubtless materially assisted in founding the chapels at Gorton and Newton, all of which, to some extent, proved beneficial to Droylsden. Humphrey Chetham, also, in one of his early wills, bequeathed £500 for the maintenance of "university men" at the chapels above named, and that will was only revoked in order to make way for the foundation of his imperishable hospital and library, which have rendered his name a venerated "household word" throughout South Lancashire. The mantle of benevolence and care for the moral and spiritual welfare of the people appears to have descended through successive owners of the Clayton estate; and the present proprietor, in addition to the erection of a pretty village school, seems likely to realise the anticipation of the oratory's simple bell, which, at least by its inscription, has long fore-shadowed the time when that little house of prayer should be followed by a substantial village church.

The late Samuel Oldham, Esq., of Oak View, Audenshaw, left funds towards the endowment of an infirmary, when erected in Ashton-under-Lyne, destined hereafter to benefit the inhabitants of Droylsden, the whole of the township being included within the sphere of its contemplated operations. The offertory money collected on sacramental Sundays in the Church, and also in the Licensed School Room at Clayton, is dispensed in charity by the clergy. Mrs. Benson, when resident in the neighbourhood, supported a charity purposely for lending linen to poor married women during their confinement. This is continued by the wife of the rector. Robert Cuthbertson, in 1683, devised £100 to the poor inhabitants of Salford, for which a reserved rent of £5 per annum was secured out of premises in Droylsden, to be distributed by the constables and churchwardens in blankets.

MILITARY AND VOLUNTEER TOPICS.

The Byrons probably led some of their Droylsden tenantry and retainers to the early French wars, where they won lasting renown. Later on, a portion of the inhabitants seem to have embraced the doctrines and policy of the Puritans, the township being slightly involved in the civil dissensions of the time of Charles I. At least, James Hulton and James Jollie, two Commonwealth officers, resided within it. There occurs also in the Manchester constable's accounts of 1643, a payment of " 8d. for fetching four horses from Fealsworth and Drylsden, to carry a pack for Sir Thomas Ffarfax."

During the rebellion of 1745, the foraging parties of the Scotch rebels on their route towards Ashton, passed through Little Droylsden, but did not penetrate into Droylsden Major. Nevertheless, the alarmed inhabitants expected them, and Thomas Birtenshaw, of Round Oak farm, now Fairfield, as a means of precaution, despatched his children for safety to a friend's house in Green-lane! He also concealed a favourite pony in a sand pit, at a short distance from his residence. The favourite, to his horror, but happily without any ill effect, neighed to the horses of the invaders as they passed along the highway, at a distance of a field or two.

Concerning the militia many incidental notices occur in the ratebooks—the first in 1768, when John Barlow, and John Brazier, acting as substitute for Abraham Beswick, were the militia men, on whose behalf the constable expended two shillings, one for a cockade, and the other for drink. Aaron Blackshaw, the following year, received three guineas from the rates whilst serving in a similar capacity. Again, in " three sevens" (1777), sundry militia expenses are recorded; and two years later the town gave a shilling and an old gun barrel in exchange for a new truncheon.

About the close of the century, when Bonaparte threatened the island with invasion, the inhabitants of Droylsden, simultaneously with their neighbours, fired with patriotism, proclaimed in their songs, that

" England never did, nor never shall,
Lie at the proud foot of a conqueror."

Then it was that the township possessed four militia guns, which are described as heavy, clumsy implements, with barrels a quarter of an inch thick, and stocks apparently sawn out of solid wood and guiltless of polish.   These muskets were stationed at frontier farms for the purpose of protecting the village, and intended to do battle with the French in case of invasion.

The militia system was revived, and clubs for providing substitutes for those ballotted were instituted both at the White Hart and the King's Head. The expenses of volunteering, recruiting, and the army of reserve fell heavily on the ratepayers.   The militia account in 1802-3 amounted to over sixteen guineas; and in the following year volunteering expenses were above fifteen pounds, whilst in addition the payments on behalf of the militia and army of reserve were more than eighty-five pounds. In the year ensuing, recruiting expenses amounted to above eleven pounds.

But military enthusiasm had spread through the country, and volunteering became the rage of the day. Considerable emulation in raising men sprang up between Nehemiah Heap, of Droylsden, and William Shawcross, of Gorton. The latter determined "to beard the lion in his den," and accordingly with fife and drum entered Droylsden, and beat up for recruits in opposition to his rival. Nehemiah Heap's, or "Th' Whitewood Soldiers," as they were dignified, met for exercise and drill in the village school, and, in lieu of muskets, were armed with wooden staves and brush stails! The Misses Robinson, of the Clockhouse, made rosettes of orange and mazarine blue, as large as butter prints, which, with their own fair hands they conspicuously placed on the volunteers' hats.

A few villagers, thirsting for distinction, joined the Medlock Vale Rifle Corps, and others sought renown by enrolling in the ranks of the Newton and Failsworth Volunteer Infantry.

For a series of years the ratebooks are heavily burdened with extraneous disbursements. In 1807-8, over thirty-three pounds was paid for militia bounties ; three years later more than twenty-five pounds to the old and ten pounds to the local militia, which also caused an expenditure in the next year, and again so late as 1814. On the 8th of April in the latter year, peace was proclaimed, and the auspicious event was celebrated with feasting and other joyous demonstrations, particularly in Fairfield, where an imposing procession, headed by a splendid new banner, passed round the settlement. But war was soon renewed, and in the year following the ratebooks record eight shillings paid to the account of the local militia at Failsworth, and a like amount expended in the purchase of four truncheons for the use of the constables.

Descending to modern times, the liberal subscriptions to the Patriotic Fund, in January, 1855, evince the warm sympathy of the people for the army when its efforts are directed in a righteous cause. The contributions in Droylsden alone realised £111 17s. 4d., of which sum the public raised £43 13s. 6d.; Edge-lane Mill, £16 12s. 7d.; Fairfield Mills, £15 16s.; Angola, £14 0s. 4d.; Victoria, £11 2s.; and Droylsden Mills, £10 12s. 11d. The announcement of

H

the re-establishment of peace with Russia was received with
lively emotions of joy, and the event was celebrated, on the
last day of May, 1856, with a tea party, speeches, and other
rejoicings, under the presidency of the rector, in the Queen-
street School Room.

POLITICAL MOVEMENTS.

An intelligent loyalty seems long to have pervaded the
district. The Moravians, on the 21st of March, 1789, commemorated by an illumination the recovery of the King
(Geo. III.) from a mental aberration.

During the French war, work was scarce and provisions
dear, flour being sixpence a pound, and potatoes a guinea per
load. Though sedition stalked through the manufacturing
districts, yet within the bosoms of many of the starving
multitude the utmost loyalty and patriotism prevailed. For
instance, "Old Jammy Grimshaw," who had woven an
entire cut whilst subsisting on three roasted potatoes and
the prospect of another, which his wife had placed on the
end of the breast beam whilst he took off his work, could
still lighten his labour with singing "Britons never, never
shall be slaves!"

Nevertheless, Droylsden evinced its desire for parliamentary and political reform by furnishing its quota of
representatives in April, 1794, to the celebrated Royton
meeting, which was ruthlessly dispersed by a loyalist mob.
Samuel Shawcross, of Droylsden, contrived to escape; but
William, his elder and less fortunate brother, was taken
prisoner to Lancaster, and did not recover his liberty until
his father had expended a large sum of money.

Passing onward to 1812, the period of the Luddite riots,
the town's authorities are discovered taking ample precau-
tions to protect life and property. On the 4th of May, thirty-
eight special constables were sworn in, and the system of
watch and ward was also introduced, the township being
patrolled during the night.

During the Chartist agitation for political reform in 1848,
considerable excitement was manifested in the village, and
its advocates met in Edward-street, in a cottage taken for

the purpose. Branches of Feargus O'Connor's Land Society and Land and Labour Bank were also established. A year or two ago, formidable looking pike heads were, at intervals, disinterred in the vacant land near Halcrow-street.

Several meetings in favour of the repeal of the corn laws were held some in the open air and others in the Queen-street School Room. The revocation of that impost was celebrated in Droylsden, on August 3, 1846, with a feast and public procession of the workpeople employed at Fairfield Mills.

Early in February of the present year, a political society was instituted, under the appellation of "The Droylsden and Audenshaw Auxiliary to the Lancashire Reformers' Union."

For the purposes of county elections, Droylsden is comprised within the polling district of Manchester, qualifying, in 1835, seventy-six, and at present one hundred and twenty-six voters. On the 3rd of last May, Messrs. Cheetham and Heywood (the latter by his representative, J. Heywood, Esq.), and on the following evening Messrs. Egerton and Legh, addressed the electors and non-electors of this district in the Droylsden Educational Institution. There is, nevertheless, an absence of virulent party feeling, and men, separated by various diversities of political opinion, otherwise freely mingle on the same platform and earnestly combine for the benefit of the public at large.

THE MOSS.

The process of moss, bog, or peat formation, is thus explained. Extensive forests, covering valleys and hill sides, are inundated, and the uprooted trees form a barrier which prevents the entire egress of the water; or trees, decayed with age, or snapped asunder by the wind, fall across a sluggish stream, and choke up the outlet. The excessive moisture kills the surrounding timber, and either the roots loosen and the trees sink and fall, or branch after branch drops down, the bole ultimately yielding to the same fate. Gradually there is formed a swamp, marsh, or morass—neither land nor water — engendering, and particularly adapted for the growth of, aquatic and semi-amphibious plants, which flourish, decay, and, in turn, are succeeded by others, until a light spongy soil is produced. The flowers, berries, and seeds of the plants, which include mosses, sedges, cotton, and other grasses, are occasionally disinterred almost as fresh as when newly fallen. Being of rapid growth, in a generation or two, as the result has proved in old marl pits, owing to the decay and subsidence of successive vegetation, and the constantly increasing pressure from above, the lower strata assumes the consistency of peat, or turf, fit for fuel. As the vegetation accumulates and becomes more compressed, the lower mass gradually becomes more dense and black, constantly approximating nearer and nearer to coal. The upper portion also gains firmness and solidity, until it attains the characteristics of a heath, moor, or common, and affords sustenance to rushes, ferns, and heather.

Ashton Moss, recently consisting of upwards of 200 acres, and once extending over probably three or four times that surface, lies chiefly in Audenshaw, but partly in Droylsden. Droylsden Moor is mentioned in 1505, and various title deeds and evidences distinctly specify that, early in the seventeenth century, moss rooms, doals, or allotments on Droylsden Moss appertained to the several farm holdings, peat being at that period the principal fuel in use. In fact, indisputable evidence remains of this boggy deposit having once overspread a very considerable portion of the east and south east sides of the township, doubtless joining the Openshaw Moss, which, though supplying fuel to the tenantry of three or four hamlets, retained, so late as the fourteenth century, a superficial area of one hundred Lancashire acres in extent. This supposition is borne out by the present appellations of fields and districts, such as Moorside, Mossside, Moorcroft, Madgefield (i.e. moor edge), &c. On the premises at Fairfield Mills, whilst digging the foundations for gas works, the workmen came upon several layers of peat, enclosed in adventitious soil, in appearance not unlike a dish of sandwiches.

The site of Fairfield, at the time of its purchase by the Brethren, is said to have been wet and marshy. Lower

down, near the Copperas Works, and also behind Annet-lane
Fold, traces of turf cutting have been distinctly found.
Bog meadows, a little further on, adjoined the Openshaw
Moss, whose confines are determined by the appellations
Moor-lane, Moorfields, &c. The ditch waters of that locality
deposit a yellowish red sediment, termed "car," a contrac-
tion of ochre. This deposit denotes the presence of carbonate
of iron, a mineral with which peat, from its vegetable
nature, is always largely imbued. The deeds of the Edge-
lane estate, in 1616, mention fields named Nearer and Further Moorfield, and Little Moorcroft; and also enumerates
"one roodland of ground as the same is now meared, severed,
divided, or taken out of or from the south west end of a
certain moore within Openshaw, called Openshaw Moore."
At that period £4 15s. was the value of a moss room containing an area of 2,000 square yards.

Through the subsidence of the water, the depth of the
peat is gradually being reduced, yet, in the centre of the
moss, where the bed remains intact, though diminished some
five feet by drainage, it still retains a thickness ranging from
twenty to twenty-four feet. Near the surface, the decayed
vegetable matter, locally designated "white turf," is lightish
brown in colour, and spongy in texture; next comes "grey
turf," full of branches, bark, and leaves of trees, greatly
inflammable and speedily consumed; then four feet of dense
black and shining peat earth; and lastly, resting on the
original surface, the remnants of stems and branches of
trees partially decomposed. This mould, or rather silt,
sometimes a coarse white sand, but usually a muddy ash-
coloured marl, tons of which have been sold to the potters,
has itself been deposited by an irruption of water. Beneath
this, at a depth of several feet, lies an unctuous, rich marl,
of much use in the reclamation of the moss. The surface
of the moss, prior to cultivation, was not more undulating
and unequal than the clayey surface below, which contained frequent hollows and depressions several feet in
depth. Beneath the foreign crust lie large quantities of
diluvial trees, the growth of centuries, at a period when
the site was dry land. Trunks of oak, birch, and hazel,

indigenous to the spot, and fir, have been periodically exhumed, but neither willow, sycamore, alder, yew, nor even
ash, once abundant in the district, have been discovered, being
perhaps of a more perishable nature. Hazel nuts have been
found, but neither acorns nor fir cones. Generally, the buried
oaks are of an ebony jet colour, firm in texture, and destitute
of symptoms of decay; but they crumble away after a few
years exposure to the atmosphere, and consequently are fit
only for fencing and fuel. The stock of an oak used for the
former purpose was discovered four or five years ago, at
"Far-end-o'th'-World"; it measured nine feet in circumference, which is the estimated growth of from two to three
centuries. Another specimen, thirty-two feet long, with end
diameters of eighteen and thirty-three inches, was found, a
few years ago, on the south side of Ashton New-road, a
little above Droylsden Church. The bark of the birch tree
still retains its silvery whiteness, notwithstanding its long
burial. Formerly splints of red fir, full of resin, were used
by the poor, in lieu of candles.

The question arises, is the moss of local or foreign formation? Clay, in his "Geological Sketches," contends that
the bog has been formed on a more elevated site, probably
Alt Hill, and, becoming surcharged with moisture, has
vacated its original site, and travelled onwards, until the
forest here existing offered sufficient resistance to determine
its settlement. Travelling bogs are not very uncommon.
Irruptions and overflowings of Hough, Chat, and Pilling
Mosses, in Lancashire, and Monteith and Solway Mosses,
in Scotland, have been recorded. Ashton Moss, lying higher
than the surrounding land, has frequently, at the "back
end" of the year, when swollen out with rains, overflowed
the fields adjacent. On one occasion, this discharge spread
half way across Joseph Howarth's meadow, and threatened
his dwelling house. As, with the increase of drainage, the
surface of the moss subsides, so objects, once concealed from
certain stand points, like Charlestown from the site of the
churchyard, are constantly becoming more and more visible.
Owing, however, to the absence of thorough drainage, the
peat in wet seasons swells out, like a sponge, diminishing

the prospect until the moisture gradually subsides. Hurricane and flood, axe and fire, may be said to have aided in the creation of the moss. Clay states that the trunks of the decayed trees lie horizontally from north east to south west; but an old Droylsden peat getter maintains they were blown down by a violent north west wind. The trees in the White Moss appear to have been hurled down by a west or north west gale of wind. In both instances, the pressure seems to have operated in one direction, as the timber is all driven down to one inclination. Another theory affirms that Ashton Moss was produced by the prostration of the primeval forest during an extraordinary inundation; and that, subsequently, some great convulsion of nature raised this marshy valley into upland, as it at present appears. Popular belief assigns its origin to the action of the great deluge, or, as old folks express it, to "th' settlin's o' Noah's flood."

Many of the tree boles are found snapped off, and lying across their stumps. The roots remain firmly fixed in the soil. Some of the trunks also exhibit unmistakable signs of destruction by fire. A huge oak, disinterred near Jacklane end, was found to be considerably charred; and at its foot lay a mass of wood ashes. There can be no doubt, then, of the local formation of the moss.

And, lastly, concerning the origin of the moss, a venerable native, who has resided on its borders all his lifetime, attributes it to the Romans during their subjugation of the country. Three Roman coins of the second century and some pottery, which rested on the natural surface, are the only products of man's skill ever discovered in the moss; and the situation of these would seem to indicate that the formation of the moss took place at a period subsequent to the irruption of the Romans. Speaking of Chat Moss, Baines (iii. p. 131) asserts that it was originally an immense forest, but reduced to a bog by the Roman invaders, at a period coeval with the first promulgation of the Christian religion. It cannot be doubted that the Romans interfered with the natural drainage, and burned the forests, on account of the shelter and covert afforded by their impenetrable recesses to the swarms of suffering Britons. But this can scarcely have been the case with the forest here existing, as the dates of the coins are posterior to the Roman conquest.

The tenant of each estate, up to about sixty years ago, possessed the right of getting fuel on a moss room, either for his own use or for sale; and he could, if he preferred, sublet a portion of the doal to the cottagers of the neighbourhood.

At some periods of the year, the moss resembled an encampment, turf stacks being scattered over the surface in every direction. But moss carts and moss barrows, turf cutters and turf fires, are now to be numbered among the things of the past. By means of draining and marling, fencing and manuring, this once wild and sullen desolation has been converted into good grazing and arable land; and at present, whilst under cereal and green crops, it surpasses in fertility the more ancient reclaimed lands by which it is surrounded.

SANITARY OBSERVATIONS.

The situation of Droylsden is open and elevated, a point near Waterside being 215 feet above the datum line of the Ordnance survey, and a still more elevated level at Moorside is above 150 feet higher than the city of Manchester. Owing to this circumstance the atmosphere has ample scope for circulation, and diseases of the respiratory organs are not so common as might be expected from the prevalence of humid exhalations.

The fall of rain in the township has not been registered; but, during the year 1852, the register indicated 37·34 inches at the Gorton Water Works, little more than a mile distant from the southern boundary of Droylsden.

In consequence of the clayey subsoil resisting the percolation of moisture, the fields after a shower often exhibit a series of temporary pools, provincially termed "laches," from which unhealthy exhalations arise. This may partly account for the "bouts" of sickness and colds which attack strangers on their first arrival, and which are grown so customary as to fail in attracting notice from any but the afflicted; nevertheless, the undulatory contour of a considerable portion of the township yields a good fall for natural drainage, which is absorbed by the Medlock and its affluents, and conduces to the general health of the inhabitants. But there is much needed a thorough system of drainage for the agricultural, and another of artificial sewerage for the populated districts. Even the latter would prove comparatively cheap and easy, as the few isolated attempts already made evince; and it would also contribute largely towards controlling preventible disease. It is certain that, as the habited space increases in extent, Droylsden will find many sanitary evils to contend with, and great difficulties to overcome, in order to replace it on a par, in health and salubrity, with its state when it contained but a rural and scattered population.

Of course, diseases arising from excessive moisture of soil and climate have long preponderated; fevers have been anything but uncommon; and a large mortality among children has prevailed. One of these latter visitations, which prevailed in the winter of 1821-2, led to the institution of a burial society in connection with the Wesleyan Sunday School. About that period, too, typhus fever virulently infested the township for nine years without intermission. Yet fever is prevented in all well regulated gaols, and the highest medical authorities declare that it may be banished from houses. During the prevalence of cholera in Britain, about ten or eleven years ago, the unanimous testimony of inspectors' and medical officers' reports announced the startling fact that cholera prevailed where fever was common.

Tradition represents that Manchester, and especially the villages in its vicinity, were visited during the seventeenth century with an epidemical or pestilential disease, which, assuming the form of a "sweating sickness," was attended with such fatal results that people could not be procured to bury the dead. The Halls, of the Clockhouse, at that time opulent bleachers, are said, in commiseration, to have despatched their men and horses, vehicles and apprentices, in order to inter those who died from the malady. A small pox visitation, in 1777, carried off at least thirteen victims in Droylsden, and thereby almost decimated the scanty population.

In olden times, before the introduction of streets, fourteen rows and dwellings ranged back to back, deficient alike in air space and ventilation. Instances of longevity were not uncommon. Five hoary headed brothers attained an aggregate age of 361 years; and Ann Grimshaw, who died in September, 1719, arrived at the patriarchal age of one hundred and one.

It has been found impracticable to obtain, separated from Audenshaw, the rate of mortality, the increase, and the nuptial engagements of the population; but the local registrar has stated, on two different occasions, the Droylsden mortality at 3 and 3½ per cent. However that may be, there is no doubt but that, by proper sanitary regulations, the yearly number of deaths in proportion to the living might be greatly reduced, and that diseases which now prevail might, as a consequence, in a few years after the removal of the predisposing causes, be entirely eradicated, and the general health of the inhabitants otherwise improved.

A number of interments have taken place at the Wesleyan Chapel; but at present the only graveyards in use are those at the Church and Fairfield Chapel. The peculiar method adopted at the latter place of single interments in graves six feet deep, if generally followed, would produce much sanitary benefit, and the extra outlay for land need scarcely exceed the sum often uselessly spent in ale and tobacco.

The few remaining old style cottages, owing to casemented windows, are sadly deficient in light, and the rooms are mostly too low. The ground floor is generally sunk beneath the surface of the land, and, in consequence of the site being either imperfectly drained or not drained at all, many complaints are made of damp walls and floors, and their moist and blackened appearance testifies to the justice of the murmuring. Some of the cottages are rendered unhealthy also from possessing no back door, or any outlet except the front entrance, and from the impossibility of opening the windows to admit fresh supplies of pure air. Unfortunately, in modern erections the lower sash alone is made to open, and hence, even in summer, little fresh air is admitted to the dwelling.

Owing to limited superficial area, many cottages are over-crowded with inmates. Health and strength cannot ordi-narily be maintained in a breathing space of less than from 700 to 800 cubic feet; and to live and sleep in a space of less than from 400 to 500 cubic feet for each individual is incompatible with safety to health and life. Some model back yard to back yard cottages in the village, with two rooms above, and as many below, possess an aggregate of less than 4,500 cubic feet. Now, a census of 28 mill cottages yielded a total of 176 persons, or an average of 6·2 occupants to each dwelling; and of the number, 56 were heads of families and children working, 78 children unemployed, and the remain-ing 42, or nearly one fourth of the entire number, were found to be lodgers. Therefore, as some of the above cramped human cages would only contain a married couple, others of necessity including lodgers must be occupied by four or five adults, besides a swarm of children and young persons. Happily, Droylsden has few cellar dwellings. The nearest approach on a large scale to that objectionable description of residence exists in Edge-lane; but, judging from the frequent recurrence of "To let," there seems little induce-ment for further speculation in that type of dwelling.

One of the greatest promotants of health and comfort is a constant and copious supply of pure water, and no benevolent improvement is more needed than this to place Droylsden in a position favourable to future development. At present the means of supply, alike for general, domestic, and culinary purposes, consists of three or four barrels, which retail water, principally obtained from Openshaw, some eight or nine pump springs, and three or four surface wells, supplemented by rain tubs and leaden cisterns, stag-nant pools, and the canal.

Wells are apt to get foul from the infiltration of impure liquids from the surface. Rain water, especially during summer, teems with animalculæ; and several cases of poisonous effects have arisen from cisterns in Droylsden.

Unfiltered canal water is unfit for use on account of the numerous deleterious influences at work on its banks. In addition, the canal is the grand absorber of most of the drainage and sewage of the locality ; and the impurity is further augmented by the putrifying animal matter which is constantly thrown therein. Lastly, the canal is the substitute, *pro tem.*, for public baths and washhouses.

Some cottages at West End are partially supplied by a stand pipe in the street from the Beswick reservoir ; and Fairfield is also an exception. More than thirty-five years ago, the Moravians erected a filter, composed of stones, river sand, and charcoal, and procured a supply of water from the proprietors of the canal. Pipes, which are monthly examined, are laid to most of the houses, and for the benefit of the rest the establishment is open during certain hours in the day.

Several attempts, dating from a public meeting held June the 18th, 1849, have been made to introduce an ample supply of water, but hitherto without effect, and the present united supplies remain casual and intermittant, as well as inadequate, expensive, and inconvenient.

Notwithstanding the imminent risk of fire in the cotton mills and other manufactories, the only fire engine at present stationed in the township is the property of the Moravians, and is located in Fairfield.

The supply of gas, both for shops and dwelling houses, was wholly derived from Fairfield Mills, excepting Fairfield, which contained the only public lights and street lamps in the village, and was supplied from Droylsden Mills. After meetings respecting the price of gas had been held in January, 1850, a joint stock company was instituted. Having purchased a site adjacent to the canal in Greenside-lane, the company erected ample retorts, gas holder, and other apparatus, and in the following October offered gas at 5s. per thousand cubic feet. Messrs. Christy reducing their price to 4s., the company fell into difficulties, and their property was finally transferred to a new company, under the Limited Liability Act, which has also purchased the public pipes and mains of Messrs. Christy.

For sanitary purposes, in October, 1853, the township was divided into four sections, and five amateur inspectors were appointed to each district. This scheme proving noperative, the sergeant of police was elected as paid inspector. A public meeting was held in the Queen-street School Room, March 22, 1854, in order to consider the propriety of introducing the Health of Towns Act into Droylsden. At the adjourned meeting, on the 24th of the month following, a motion for its adoption was defeated by 113 voting for, and only 20 against, an adjournment *sine die*. Nevertheless the agitation produced salutary effects; and amongst other improvements expedited were the removal of obstructions from the *trotoirs* and flagging them, paving portions of the highways, and the construction of sewers. Still, a cursory survey of the village reveals a large number of open drains, sinks, ditches, cesspools, and sewers, generating large quantities of carbonic acid gas, which, besides emitting a most disagreeable odour, is highly detrimental to health and destructive to life.

Thunder storms have frequently visited the township. Trees have been struck, and both men and cattle have perished by the electric fluid. One Ogden, a farm servant, and three cows, were killed by lightning, in August, 1851, in a shippon at Clayton.

REMEDIAL SANITARY MEASURES.

As when cholera, influenza, fevers, or contagious disorders break out in a place, more people die in the dark, damp, and dirty streets, than in those parts which are light, clean, and airy, so more cleanly habits, better food, good clothing, good lodging, and other comforts, coupled with better cultivation and drainage of the land as well as streets, would eradicate many predominant causes of disease. At present, nuisances exist even around isolated cottages and farmsteads, to say nothing of new blocks of dwellings which are constantly being erected. These nuisances are occasionally temporarily removed, or abated for a time; but, as private individuals are too apathetic or powerless for good, there is no provision made for their entire eradication, either by permanent works or by the active attention of proper servants; and, consequently, they are continually recurring.

Most of the new streets and thoroughfares are impassable for wheeled vehicles, for want of paving and sewering. In order to remedy this evil there ought to be a local governing body, possessing summary power in case of refusal. Every street and road should be swept, and the dust collected, once or twice a week; and no scavengers' heaps, or other offensive matter, should be suffered to remain in the streets, or near where human beings are congregated. Slaughter houses, piggeries, and chemical works ought to be removed from inhabited districts. Accumulations of decomposing dead animal and vegetable matter, dung, manure, middens, ashpits, open and covered cesspools, privies, and stagnant ditches—reeking with the refuse from adjoining houses—ought to be removed forthwith, as this state of things can only grow worse, and must become more difficult, as well as more expensive, to remedy, as the agricultural lands become absorbed in the township. In addition to all back yards being well flagged or paved, careful attention ought to be paid to the sewerage of every habitation; and where drains are too large or expensive, tile pipe drains of small diameter might be employed. Water closets separated from the houses should supersede privies and cesspools, and should be connected with the street drains, and discharge themselves into sewers of transmission, and not of deposit. In dry seasons these ought to be periodically flushed; in wet weather this is unnecessary, a copious shower of rain ever being a great sanitary blessing. In case of à thorough system of drainage, there are various falls and water sheddings which would be available for the erection of tanks, as at Fairfield, but proportionably larger, and a depôt for the collection and condensation of the manure, which might be turned to a profitable use by neighbouring agriculturalists.

Every street should be lighted with gas during dark nights; and, above all, a copious supply of the best water obtainable should be forthwith supplied at the lowest cost to every house in the village. The water should be supplied to the dwellings, and not by stand pipes in the street; for the former method, besides being more convenient, is found, also, to be more economical.

All the canal bridges, with, perhaps, a single exception, want widening; the names of the streets should be placed in conspicuous positions; and the doors of dwelling houses should be numbered forthwith.

Finally, some portion of the Recreation Ground should be planted with shrubs and trees, and interspersed with walks and promenades, as well for pleasure as exercise. It is much cheaper to provide rational pastimes than to punish crime; and if people are encouraged in active and healthful recreation, the disposition towards crime will be greatly diminished.